MW01145317

WITH WARMEST REGARDS
TO ANN CRISWELL —
FOR A LONGTIME FRIENDSHIP,
AND SINCERE THANKS FOR
YOUR SUPPORT —

Erik Jonhck

APRIL 2, 2008

# At Your Service

# At Your Service

## A Journey from Bohemia to Texas

### by Erik Worscheh
### with Beverly Harris

Copyright © 2008 by Erik Worscheh

All rights reserved. No part of this book may be reproduced or transmitted in any form or by any means, electronic or mechanical, including photocopying, recording or by any information storage and retrieval system, without written permission from Erik Worscheh, except for the inclusion of brief quotations in a review.

FIRST EDITION
ISBN 13: 978-1-931823-65-4

Printed in USA

*Front cover photo courtesy of*
GenesisPhotographers.com

**Designed and Produced by**
Kingsley Literary Services
2656 S. Loop W. Suite 440
Houston, Texas 77054
www.kingsleybooks.com
713-771-1514

*To Mary*
*with all my love*

# Acknowledgements

I can't thank my dear wife, Mary, enough for her support and efforts on this project. Many friends suggested I do something with my collection of documents. They detail my journey from Bohemia to Texas and my experiences in America with people of greatness. These included Presidents, financiers, space explorers, entertainers and the outstanding staffs of several luxury hotels and clubs.

It was Mary who gave the "go" signal, and then kept my enthusiasm and memory in top form. It was her advice to find an experienced writer to put my words down in a "story telling" fashion. Through friends Carter Rochelle and Ann Criswell, we met Beverly Harris, a former Lifestyle editor and feature writer for the *Houston Chronicle*. Having also watched Houston in the years it found sophistication in tastes, lifestyles, entertainment and fine dining, Beverly appreciated my reactions and contributions.

I owe much to son Mark and his wife, Sue. Both encouraged me to tell my story as a bequest for their three delightful daughters. I like to think that Hannah, Sophie and Amy will marvel at these details of Papa's life—a life that sometimes presented more challenges than necessary, but invariably was interesting and rewarding.

—EJW

# Contents

# Central Europe, 1918 - 1945

# Introduction

*I*f by magic one afternoon you could turn the clock back to 1935 and look down on the village of Jechnitz, Czechoslovakia, you might hear the frantic scraping and swishing of skates on a frozen lake. You might also hear boys shouting in exuberant German as they maneuvered a hockey puck toward the goalkeeper. Finally, when the sun's warmth yielded to shadows and allowed winter's chill to settle over the town, you'd notice the noise moderated somewhat. You'd watch the boys, cheeks flushed and energy abated, gather their gear and walk toward a tree-lined avenue made elegant by decorative stones in a swirled pattern.

The tallest boy would be Erik. He and his younger brother, Walter, skates dangling over their shoulders, weren't headed for an ordinary house. Their home was the highly regarded, dignified Hotel Worschech. It belonged to their parents, Alfred and Franziska (née Buresch) Worschech, known to their children as Papa and Mutti.

Erik as usual had several things on his mind but foremost a fine meal, and when one lived in the best hotel in town, there was no other kind. He'd find his methodical mother in the kitchen supervising the staff, and his easygoing father in the back, directing the butchering of fine quality meats.

Their fresh and natural food—today we'd label it organic—lured guests from ancient Prague, capital city of spires 60 miles from Jechnitz, and from other points in Czechoslovakia and even surrounding countries. One gentleman stayed at the hotel because it was adjacent to a forest where he annually collected wild mushrooms. Then there was the lady who stayed for two months at a time. She asked that her room be decorated to specifications for each visit—fresh paint and newly-stenciled flowers on the walls. Her wishes were granted. It

Hotel ⬛. Schule    Jechnitz am See

*Hotel Worschech in Jechnitz drew guests from miles away. Papa and Mutti pampered them all, even changed décor at their request. Years later, Erik returned and was heart-broken to find it devastated by communist rule.*

was a close, innocent world with no apprehensions, no awareness of a disaster in the making.

The Worschech children, including little sister Margit, experienced the good life. They had devoted parents, comfortable quarters, fine tailored clothing, excellent schooling and private music lessons. Their father had been a member of Kaiser Franz Joseph's service staff in Vienna. Their mother's occupational dossier would include her time as governess for a British aristocrat.

The parents believed in character-building discipline. As in all families, however, there were occasional mishaps. Erik's earliest memory was of pushing his baby sister's pram for a wintery walk. About five years old at the time, he couldn't resist turning off solid ground to continue the stroll on the frozen lake. Suddenly his feet slipped from under him. Instead of taking the fall alone, he gripped the handle with all his

*The Worschech brothers, Walter, left, almost a year old, and Erik, age two. When Erik came to the U.S., he simplified the spelling of his surname by eliminating the second "c."*

strength. The carriage flipped backward with force. Baby Margit sailed out of her snug quarters, arched over Erik's head and thumped down on the ice. By a miracle, her winter clothing softened the impact. But the trauma Erik felt etched a lasting memory in his young mind.

Erik's mischievous expression still reflects the chagrin he experienced on another occasion when he and his brother skidded across the hotel's slick parquet floor in their socks, pretending to be on skates. Using a tennis ball as a puck, Erik gave his hockey stick a mighty swing. The puck sailed with shattering force into one of the hotel's tall mirrors, canceling all elegance. Punishment was equally swift. Papa Worschech grabbed young Walter and applied his hand, unaware that he had the lesser culprit. Erik later confessed and took the consequences. But at least they were spared the wrath of Mutti. Mrs. Worschech, a loving woman but strict disciplinarian, responded to unruly behavior by reaching into a particular

*Erik, Walter and little sister Margit in typical dressy attire. They lived in the refined atmosphere of the family hotel in Jechnitz, Czechoslovakia.*

kitchen drawer for the dreaded *kochloffel*, a long and sturdy wooden spoon with which she demonstrated her own athletic swing.

The boys, who shared a bedroom upstairs—hotel procedure labeled it Number Five—found it difficult to simply recline for the night. An armoire at the foot of their bed beckoned a ritual. They liked to vault over the tall furniture and crash down on the other side to the goose down cover. If that wasn't enough, they sometimes used the bedside telephone to call the kitchen below. It had no voice facility, but such a call made the room number flash downstairs and soon a servant interrupted work to answer the frivolous summons. Lo and behold, quite often the "servant" turned out to be Mutti with the *kochloffel*.

Giving in to a little smile, Erik remembers how he often pointed blame at Walter for various wrongdoings. "But after the war, it was the other way around. He came home and gave *me* orders." Other than a few such misadventures, the children caused their parents little worry. Erik aced mathematics, and languages were no problem at all—being Czechoslovakian cinched that. He already knew German, the language spoken at home. He studied Czech and French in school, and picked up a bit of Russian and English. He could tell from which part of Middle Europe a person came by his dialect. With such

4

abilities, his consuming dream was to go into diplomatic service.

Aside from formal studies, Erik showed real talent for painting, violin, accordion and piano. One of his music teachers was a remarkable man Erik remembers as Herr Gareis, a peerless example of multi-tasking. In exchange for room and board at the hotel, he gave the children piano lessons, helped them with homework, greeted guests arriving at the train station (after walking the

*Approaching their teens, brothers Walter, left, and Erik had a full schedule of sports, music, serious studies and occasional mischief.*

mile distance along with the baggage handler and his pull-cart) and playing the baby grand in the hotel Kaffee Haus on weekday evenings. On weekends, a trio took the music assignment. Occasionally Erik joined the little band. Erik remembers being annoyed (that's his story) by flirty girls who ruffled his hair and giggled as they danced by, and since his hands were fully occupied with the accordion, he had to *oom-pah* steadily on with hair falling over his eyes.

So Erik forever had much on his mind. But not in his wildest dreams could he imagine how his idyllic world would someday shatter like that hotel mirror. How could it possibly happen that his family would be missing for two years, that the hotel itself would be lost, and that Erik would find himself on first one side, then the opposite of a world conflict? Nor could he have imagined that years later his life would be reborn on the other side of the world where even his name would be spelled differently.

*Before the storm clouds—smiling Walter, Margit and Erik could never have imagined how their idyllic lives would be torn apart by World War II.*

*Erik on the accordion enjoying a songfest with family; from left: Margit, Papa, Mutti, and friends.*

# Chapter One
## An Abrupt Change of Plans

*A*t the urging of his family and friends, Erik Worscheh sat down one day to prepare an outline of his life. He was getting up in years—was it his intention, they had asked, to drift off into the retirement sunset without leaving some written details of his remarkable itinerary and professional accomplishments?

He thought it over. Previously he'd been entirely too busy—on his feet for hours every day, managing, directing—to care about eulogizing himself. But now that his six-foot-four frame leaned on a cane and his energy nagged him to sink into a comfortable chair, he gave the matter of perpetuating his memories some respect.

The problem was his acute sense of organization and brevity, honed by military service and a long career in food

*Still together in happier times before WWII—front row, Mutti, Erik and Papa Worschech; in back, Margit and Walter.*

and beverage management. Even he realized that his finished "memoir" had the tone of a chronological worksheet designed to galvanize a major hotel's kitchen staff.

It began:

> *Birthplace and early Data:*
> *Born on Sunday, Dec. 23, 1922 in Weseritz-Bohemia, Czechoslovakia near towns of Budweis, Pilsen and Michelob, home of world's best hops. Mother Franziska Buresch, Father, Alfred Worschech. Education: Early school-Podersam-Saaz; Middle school-Karlsbad and Prague Academy; College-University of Nurnberg. Hotel Training: Grand Hotel Pupp, Grand Hotel Imperial in Karlsbad, 1936-1938.*
>
> *In 1939, Germany occupied Czechoslovakia. Was studying in Karlsbad. Drafted into Workforce, "Arbeitsdienst" in 1940.*
>
> *Drafted into the German navy. After training, assigned to a minesweeper headed to the North Sea and Baltic Sea.*

The terse outline doesn't mention Adolf Hitler. It passes lightly over changes in lifestyle that the führer and later the Communists brought about. But Erik doesn't hesitate to describe the events orally in vivid detail.

People have asked, he said, why citizens of Sudetenland, the German-speaking regions of Bohemia and Moravia, Czechoslovakia, didn't resist Germany in September of 1938. At first the occupation was smooth and bloodless. Locals in this area bordering Germany already spoke the invaders' language and by all accounts, it was better to be a part of Deutschland than of Russia, a strong-armed politic they feared. In all of history, Middle European countries have been highways of invasion by one conqueror or another—where was the surprise? Although dissension roiled in sections of Czechoslovakia, many ordinary, peaceful people in the German-speaking sector felt that life would go on.

But changes persisted. The *Arbeitsdienst*, for instance. Youngsters drafted into this German-controlled compulsory workforce strained over seemingly pointless tasks, the idea being to give them a taste of harsh military life. Erik shoveled dirt into a wheelbarrow and pushed it for two miles. He dumped it and repeated the process throughout the day until he and his teen-aged coworkers created a useless mountain.

*Seaman Erik Worschech, age 18, newly drafted into the German Navy along with many other German-speaking youths from the Bohemian region of Czechoslovakia.*

On his eighteenth birthday, the assignment turned far more serious. At that age all able youth in the occupied north got drafted into Hitler's war machine. His assignment was the German navy. He never expected to be involved with the high seas. But on thinking it over, he decided the navy at least provided more comfort than the army ever gave its soldiers—better food, a covered place to sleep and relative safety.

With cherished plans for higher education and diplomacy abruptly curtailed, Erik went into World War II without the equipment of hate or greed. He was not involved in politics; he was not a Nazi. His heart spoke a different language. "I never thought of America as my enemy," he said. By serving at sea, he was isolated from German atrocities during the war.

*Moving up—Lt. Worschech was ordered to command a minesweeper/landing (rescue) boat.*

His parents still operated the hotel; their letters got through, so family life, though altered, did go on.

Military training, whatever the country, can have a lasting effect on character and ability, hence the old concept, "He went into the service a boy and came out a man." Erik's mind, already sharpened by the disciplines of mathematics and music, developed a heightened sense of organization which in turn prepared him for positions of authority. The navy recognized those leadership qualities and in time he moved up the ranks to lieutenant and command of his own vessel. His assignment was to comb the North Sea, which in winter amounted to a treacherous *danse macabre* through wind and ice while detonating found mines.

On one memorable occasion, with the boat slanting at a 45 degree angle first one way and then the opposite, his steward approached the bridge carrying another steaming mug of coffee. Erik welcomed these frequent gestures—the coffee warmed his insides before they could freeze.

But he was curious. "How is it that you can get a full mug of coffee up here without spilling it?"

The steward stiffened. "I will tell you if you promise not to punish me."

Odd, thought Erik, but he agreed.

The steward explained: At the bottom steps he always felt the reeling and jerking as the boat struggled ahead. He knew he couldn't make it up to the bridge without a spill. So, hot as it was, he slurped a big amount of coffee into his mouth and held it there until he approached the bridge. Then he opened his mouth and returned the coffee to its mug. Erik was stunned. All this time he'd been drinking recycled beverages! It took a while, but he finally dismissed revulsion and an insulted stomach, and conceded that the coffee had tasted quite good.

Less amusing is his memory of seeing a Russian torpedo headed straight for his minesweeper. Only by using all his strength to steer the vessel to one side did he avoid collision—the torpedo cruised by a mere ten feet away.

"I got a lot of hoorays from the crew for that one."

And he tells how the crew tipped depth charges overboard, their targets being suspected enemy submarines. "It was our mission; we had to do this." They felt the explosions and once saw debris, a sign of a hit. "But we couldn't be sure." Erik's soft tone suggests that he didn't want to be sure, that he preferred to think of rescue missions rather than destruction.

What was ahead, though, was all too identifiable. Erik was soon to see the monstrous face of real conflict. This would come not during the war but after peace was declared.

# Chapter Two
## The Worschech Family Vanishes

Erik's personal outline continues, still only hinting at the real drama:

> *Served in flotilla under command of Admiral Sonnabend as youngest Lt. of a minesweeper. Swept mines in the North Sea and the Baltic Sea, following a general route off the German coast from the ports of Kiel and Danzig, up to the Bay of Riga, Latvia, and then to Helsinki and Kotka, Finland, searching back and forth. Whenever a mine was cut under the water, it popped to the surface and was shot with a machine gun to explode.*
>
> *March '45, Admiral moved flotilla towards the West as he did not want to fall into Russian hands and turn over secret specialized equipment to the Russians. We all felt he sympathized with British.*
>
> *March, '45. Flotilla surrendered to British. Those with no affiliation with Nazi party were separated and screened and continued to serve under British Command, in the Baltic and North Seas, 1945-47.*
>
> *After war, Russia occupied Czechoslovak Socialist Republic (CSR). Had no contact with family. Tried through Geneva to locate parents and family.*

Before the war ended, Admiral Sonnabend directed his fleet of seven minesweepers toward the small countries of Latvia, Estonia and Lithuania on the Baltic Sea. Cradled by Russia, these countries held many desperate people who wanted out. If they stayed, entire families likely would perish. Imagine their relief when they spotted the German vessels sailing toward their shore. Hundreds, not only Germans but

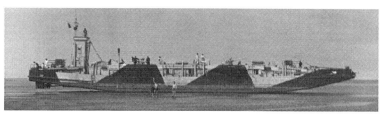

*A typical German minesweeper/landing vessel during World War II. Its job (and Erik's) was to detonate explosives in the icy waters of the Baltic Sea and rescue refugees fleeing Latvia and Estonia.*

also Estonians, Lithuanians and Latvians, pushed to get on board for passage to Danzig, which then was a part of Germany.

Sometimes the rescue went smoothly, but Erik remembers an agonizing event. As soon as the landing ramp was lowered for access, so many refugees crushed forward that there was barely space left to breath. Still there were people in panic to get on board, but they were ordered to stay put while the roadway was hauled up. Nevertheless, three or four men made a terrible decision: they clung to the raised ramp. Without a doubt, they would lose their grip and plunge into the freezing water. One of Erik's crew members raised his gun and fired, saving the desperate men from a slower death by drowning. Not long after the boat began its journey, refugees suffered from bitter cold and hunger. "Half of them didn't make it," said Erik.

On another run, the ethnic mix of refugees reached Danzig, their hope for freedom, but the Russians anticipated the arrival. Just as Erik's boat pulled away from the harbor, Russian planes dipped over the crowd and dropped a bomb. "They didn't bother with us," said Erik, who still wonders at his good fortune. "I think they just wanted to punish their people for leaving."

One day the crew eased into the Danzig harbor to see the remains of a bombed hospital ship. Dumped bodies at least ten layers high formed a ghastly pile on the stone pier. "One man was still alive but his body was torn open," said Erik. He has never been able to erase that grotesque scene from his mind.

Shortly before the flotilla's Admiral Sonnabend surrendered to the British, Erik experienced misfortune. He had just picked up a large number of refugees with the intention of delivering them to Danzig, some distance from the Russians. "We had engine problems and our boat fell out of the formation of seven. The leading ship signaled that they couldn't help. They had to abandon us," Erik said. His crippled vessel drifted for hours until it finally plowed into a sandbar about 200 feet offshore of East Prussia. It came to rest at a slant. Water surged on board in frigid waves. Soon the boat groaned under heavy ice. By six in the morning, darkness lifted just enough to see the faint outline of land and a gathering of people ready to rescue. Erik gave the command to abandon ship. But how?

A signal from land told them to be alert and ready for a lifeline from the shore. It needed to be caught and fastened to the minesweeper.

The procedure succeeded. One at a time, passengers grabbed a pulley, waited to be securely tied and then reeled to land. This method seemed workable, except that the individual hanging on for the ride would at one point be dragged under freezing water.

Last to leave was Erik. His trip through the water almost ended his life. To this day he only knows that he went unconscious and woke up in a hospital. He never learned how many—or how few—refugees survived. He remembers he had a high fever, which probably explains why he can't recall many details of his transfer from the hospital to a small German navy camp.

*After the war, Erik volunteered to serve as First Officer on a larger minesweeper, a German vessel under British command.*

He does remember one certainty: "I was happy to be alive."

Another obvious point: The language Erik heard was not German, but English. The camp now belonged to the British. World War II was on the verge of ending.

When it came his time to be screened by a British officer, Erik was sharp enough to answer in English. His experience on a minesweeper impressed the officer. Was Erik a member of the Nazi party? No. Any political affiliations? No. His responses sounded good to the British, who needed his kind of experience to clear the waters of more mines.

It wasn't uncommon during this recovery period for Allies to employ knowledgeable members of the opposition who knew their own land and sea transport systems, in this case, the waters and harbors. So under the British authority, a minesweeper commanded by a German named Krueger, and with Erik Worscheh second in command, again took to the sea.

World War II ended in 1945, but for many it was just beginning. Now retribution erupted. The Czech Republic declared a policy of no mercy toward the ethnic Germans living in the border regions. Erik lost communication with Mutti and Papa, Walter and Margit. He called the hotel, but there was no answer. He learned the Germans were being expelled and he despaired that his family might be sent to the Russian zone and executed. Reports coming in detailed horror stories that later were documented—women and children herded onto a bridge where the mothers were ordered to throw their children over the rail into the Elbe River; then all were shot. One report had ethnic Germans digging their own graves before taking bullets. Death marches, starvation and disease destroyed lives in acts of revenge.

Taking all that in, Erik's expectation for the future went dead. "You forget about home. Your life doesn't mean a thing any more."

For the next two years, he served under British command and tried to avoid thinking about the past, about all that was lost.

# Chapter Three
## When Better Isn't Good Enough

*E*rik's search for his family, missing for two years, had him on the telephone calling Geneva, Switzerland, where records listed names of displaced persons. Sadly, Worschech was not among them. His outline continued:

> *May, '47, on weekend leave in Hamburg. At tramway station, girl with shorn head approached and asked, "Are you Erik Worschech from Jechnitz?" I said, yes, and she said she saw our name on a refugee list at the train station in Ansbach, Bavaria. I learned that the Communists had taken over the hotel and my parents, who did not want to become Communists, were expelled to Germany. I was too excited to ask her name or where she lived. Rushed back to ship, asked for extended leave.*
>
> *To train, carrying cigarettes and food, and traveled three days on various trains, and walked over fourteen miles carrying suitcase, found parents as refugees living in a German home in Leutershausen, Germany. This was on Mother's Day, 1947.*

Mutti couldn't believe her eyes when she opened the door. She cried out. Her hands grabbed his shoulders, his arms, his chest, to help her realize it was really her son. She had prayed for so long, asking that Erik had survived the war and its bloody aftermath. Fresh on her mind were the many young men of the region who, in declaring opposition to communism, had been lined up against a wall and shot.

How they all talked during that visit! Erik learned all the grim details of their exile. Perhaps the bitterest was the story

*17*

that one of Hotel Worchech's own employees turned communist and forced the owners out. He ordered Papa to the menial job of street sweeping. Further orders stuffed them and fellow citizens into a cattle car for exile to the American zone of Germany.

Because Margit spoke Czech, she escaped the persecution inflicted on other German-speaking citizens of Sudetenland. She even got a job at NARODNI VYBOR, the Czech-controlled national committee which spelled out the new order. She gained trust, then used her relative freedom of movement by making a bold move in 1946. Margit left Jechnitz by train for Rehau, a small village about 20 kilometers from the border. En route, she quietly spoke to other refugee passengers. They made and carried out a dangerous plan. Individually they left the train and walked in extremely cold weather toward an area south of Eger.

Here they encountered an American soldier on patrol who abruptly turned the refugees back across the border. Only Margit was able to address him in English. His response was friendly, but he noticed her warm gloves and gold wristwatch. Those articles would be her price for safety. Margit then continued walking on to Selb, Germany. Her hands were nearly frozen but her heart held hope. In Selb, she finally located her distraught brother, Walter. They spent hours talking about what had happened to the family and wondering what the future would hold.

American occupation required that German families take in refugees. Papa, Mutti, Margit and a cousin were assigned to one room of a house some distance from the small town of Leutershausen. A stove in the center vented out the window so they could cook their meager rations in the cramped room without being overcome by smoke.

Erik's outline begins to show more promise at this point:

> *Returned to ship and asked for release from navy and British Command.*
> *Returned to Ansbach. Found job in Nurnberg in the Palace of Justice Building working for U.S. Military Headquarters, PBX, Dept. W., and became assistant to Mr. Linahan, purchasing agent for European Command*
> *Entered University of Nurnberg, attending class at night and off-days. After three years, applied for emigration to the United States. Sister Margit had married U.S. Air Force captain who was stationed at March Air Force Base in Riverside, CA. He became my sponsor.*

Erik found his new workplace more than merely interesting. The Nuremberg trials of Nazi war criminals such as Goering and Hess ground on for several years in the same building, The Palace of Justice. (One of the criminal prosecutors was Houston's Leon Jaworski—a picture of Erik with Jaworski hangs in the Worscheh den.)

Meanwhile, his parents and many relatives emerged from exile to start life over in Ansbach. They found a small restaurant that begged attention and threw all their energy into it. Papa cruised the countryside on his bicycle, looking for fresh eggs, milk and chickens. Mutti cooked. They

*A civilian again, Erik took a job as assistant to the PBX purchasing agent for U.S Headquarters in Nuremburg.*

*Mutti and Papa in Ansbach
prior to a train trip.*

named the place *Der Neuer Weg*, The New Way. In time, it became enormously successful. Margit found a job—actually much more than a job—at the U.S. Air Force Base in Ansbach. Her special find was an American, Capt. James (Jimmy) Fox. Their love story began in Ansbach, continued in New Rochelle, NY, where they were married, and moved to Riverside in Southern California.

In addition to working fulltime and studying, Erik helped his parents at their restaurant on weekends. But he became restless despite having a good job and, once again, fashionable tailored clothing. Every minute of his life was occupied with one consuming activity or another. All this aside, he couldn't ignore that he was a displaced person. He needed stability, a comfortable sense of belonging. The thought of emigration entered his mind, and one day he put in his application. Erik seriously considered going to Australia at the urging of a friend, but since Margit was already in the U.S., America beckoned.

Now he needed a sponsor. After correspondence back and forth, his brother-in-law in New Rochelle, N.Y., volunteered to take on that responsibility. Then there was the matter of emigrant occupations, which were carefully regulated by quota. Already there were plenty of mechanics and factory workers and the like. Erik had only one choice left. No matter all his prior naval experience, his education, his linguistic talents, his nice wardrobe—he would have to sign on as a housekeeper! While he knew there would be a wait, he didn't expect it to be quite so short. Approval and a departure schedule came awkwardly a month before his graduation. He must have provided a stellar description of his dilemma because an understanding university and the presiding Dr. Bergler granted his BA degree ahead of schedule.

*A weekend reunion in Ansbach with Mutti was a treat for Erik.*

He'd go by train to Bremerhaven where a massive Kaiser ship waited to load some two thousand refugees of many nationalities. Erik gave his distraught Mutti a final hug. She made the sign of the cross when he picked up his suitcase and left with Papa, who accompanied him to the Ansbach station.

When Erik tries to recall his farewell to Papa near a steaming, pulsing train that day, his voice chokes and he stops talking for a while. Papa ached for him to stay, but knew that his ambitious son had made up his mind and there was no point in pleading. Instead, said Erik, "He simply wished me good luck and said, 'In God's name.'"

There had been too many good-byes, too much pain. A part of Erik wanted to hold on to Papa and Mutti and never let anything bad happen to them again. Yet here he was, leaving for the other side of the world, and making them both cry.

# Chapter Four
## One-Way Fare to California

Erik added to his outline:

*As a displaced person, I received notice to report to Bremerhaven, Germany, to board the transport ship* General Hahn *for departure on November 11, 1951.*

*Because of my navy background, I became the chief of police on the ship; a fellow refugee, Dr. Michaelis, became ship doctor. We were the only persons given a cabin on the bridge. I was assigned to organize the duties of food preparation and clean-up during the seven-day trip. All information had to be given in several languages.*

*We had several dance contests on board.*

*As we passed the Statue of Liberty in New York harbor, it was a joyous scene with everybody crying in gratitude.*

*Arrived in N.Y. with five dollars in pocket, a place to stay with my brother-in-law's family in New Rochelle.*

*A few days after arrival, I walked from 1 St. to 101 St. in Manhattan, just to absorb the feel of America.*

*Had brief job at Waldorf Astoria until I saved money to go to California. In addition I borrowed $90 from my brother-in-law, which I paid back.*

Yes, dance contests! Merriment! Sailing between two worlds, life on board the massive Kaiser ship "General Hahn" reacted to a carefree interim. If anyone gave in to serious thinking during those seven days, the topics would be not so much about what was left behind as what lay ahead.

Erik's background, his penchant for organization and authority—and perhaps his commanding stature—earned him authority over the floating city. He expected every able-bodied passenger to take on a duty, from peeling potatoes to food service to trash pick-up. He took reports from each deck supervisor and made quick suggestions to cover all problems—including accidents and an epidemic of seasickness.

If that exposure didn't get him recognized by all, his next accomplishment certainly did.

Swirling and dipping a lively Italian beauty around the floor, Erik won first place in the dance contest. He still has the ribbon that proclaimed him "Mr. Hahn."

The mood changed on arrival. When the *General Hahn* eased toward the Statue of Liberty, refugees crowded the top deck to watch, most with tears glistening. For them, freedom was not a casual word. It was an apprehensive but fiercely hopeful look into the future.

Immigrants were processed through Ellis Island with amazing efficiency despite their numbers. Finished with entry requirements, Erik spotted Margit's father-in-law who had been waiting to escort him to the ferry and, in a sense, to a whole new life.

On Manhattan Island, Erik could hardly stop walking and staring at the skyscrapers. Even so, two things about his new land reconnected him to the Old Country. He couldn't believe what he saw in the windows of antiques shops—the same kind of old beat-up furniture that Mutti had stored out of sight in the hotel attic. Here they wanted fancy money for the junk.

Second, he noticed signs advertising Pilsner, Budweiser and Michelob beers, all named after towns in his former country. And that reminded him of Papa, who liked to take charge of the wine and beer cellar in the hotel. It seemed Papa had to descend those stairs frequently to check the temperature of the barrels and to taste, but he occasionally stayed too long and tasted a little too much. He'd spend the rest of the afternoon asleep on a corner chair.

"People thought poor Papa was worn out, that he worked too hard," Erik says now, and he smiles. "You see, everybody liked Papa. He was generous. He'd give everything away if Mutti let him. People didn't like Mutti as much. She was strict; she kept the pencils sharpened, did all the paper work, and kept close watch on Papa."

Erik headed for the famous Waldorf-Astoria Hotel where he applied for a job. He needed to earn one-way fare to California where his sister Margit and her husband Jimmy waited. The Waldorf could easily have been impressed with Erik's background, which included an internship (paid by his family) at Hotel Pupp, one of Europe's most elegant establishments. Indeed, he was hired immediately—as a kitchen steward. His earnings, plus borrowed cash from Jimmy's relatives at New Rochelle, got him on that plane and gave him a look at first-stop Chicago.

"I was so surprised," he said. "It was a beautiful city." He'd been influenced by Chicago's reputation for lawlessness, and expected to hear gunshots and sirens.

Back on the four-prop plane, he gazed down in fascination as America drifted by. But Los Angeles stunned him. "I never saw such a blue sky in November." Sunshine, palm trees, flowers—he thought he was in heaven.

And avocados—holding the dark leathery-skinned fruit for the first time, he asked, "Do you expect me to eat that?" Grapefruit was also new to him, but Margit produced a cookbook that gave him ideas for all kinds of California cuisine. They came in handy on his first major American job as pantry man and *garde manger*.

Riverside is home to the historic Mission Inn which opened in 1903. It draws a stream of celebrities who either check in for a stay—actress Betty White and her mother lived there—or stop by on their way to Palm Springs. President Richard Nixon and Patricia Ryan were married there in 1940 and numerous weddings and receptions ensued. The castle-like building with its labyrinth of gardens and towers, graceful Spanish arches and stairways, takes up an entire block. It has several dining areas, including a patio where romantic balconies spill lush bougainvillea.

But the Inn never knew European classic elegance until Erik Worscheh stepped into the picture. Once he got past the avocado barrier, Erik moved from pantry work to chief steward, ever upward until he became banquet manager and maitre d'hotel, a position that meant he'd work "up front" greeting the public. Locals and celebrities alike waited in the lobby until twelve noon sharp when he

*When Erik advanced to maitre d'hotel at the Mission Inn he introduced the area's casual citizens to a new level of European-style formality and elaborate service.*

dramatically opened the main dining room door for personal welcome and lunch. There he stood in splendid midday attire—a gray weskit, black coat, gray striped trousers, handkerchief in pocket and a fresh boutonniere. Against the wall at military attention stood all the wait staff, uniformly dressed and holding carefully folded napkins over left arms. A fresh bouquet scented each table. Evening meals, softened by candlelight, offered the same drama, except that Erik's outfit was even more formal. It was the Hotel Pupp all over again. Guests loved it.

A measure of his popularity occurred in 1955 when he resigned to accept a position at the new Beverly Hilton in Los Angeles. Members of his Mission Inn staff herded him into a car one day and drove to a large private home which was strangely dark. Suddenly lights flashed on and nearly two hundred people, including city officials, showered him with greetings and good wishes. A live band blared out while the crowd roared "For he's a jolly good fellow." It might please survivors of that jubilance to know Erik still gets emotional when he recounts the event.

## Inn's 'Mr. Erik' Takes Post at Beverly Hilton

The Mission Inn's "Mr. Erik," main dining room manager for two years and functionary of the hotel since February of 1952, has taken a position with the new Beverly Hilton Hotel in Beverly Hills.

Employes of the Inn recently staged a surprise farewell party for him and gave him a gift of luggage.

"Mr. Erik," born in Czechoslovakia, came to America late in 1951 after a career in European hotels.

*A June, 1955, issue of a Riverside newspaper notes that the Mission Inn's "Mr. Erik" was lured away by the posh new Hilton hotel in Beverly Hills.*

An unexpected intermission between Riverside and Los Angeles jobs, due to hotel construction delays, had Erik working as maitre d' at the Royal Nevada Hotel in Las Vegas for six months. He met many a celebrity there, including Frank Sinatra and the Rat Pack. When the Beverly Hilton, the nation's first new luxury hotel after World War II, finally got everything nailed in place, Erik was notified to come back to Los Angeles. But upon arrival, he discovered that all major positions were filled, employees having been siphoned off from the Waldorf-Astoria. The only position open was assistant room service manager. It sounded so ordinary after the Mission Inn.

Visitors of note wanting the feel of Los Angeles glamour gravitated to the fabulous Beverly Hilton. However, they preferred to avoid the gawking public. To Erik's surprise, his job included service to busy private dining rooms for luncheons, normally the function of the banquet catering office. Suddenly he was attending to celebrities and notables, President Harry S. Truman among them. He learned to be at ease around such as Bob Hope, Elizabeth Taylor, Milton Berle, Dr. Robert Schuler, Red Skelton, Clark Gable, Danny Thomas, John Wayne, Jerry Lewis, Debbie Reynolds, Henry J. Kaiser, Edsel Ford and Howard Hughes.

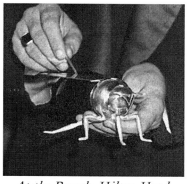

*At the Beverly Hilton Hotel, Erik holds a silver honey pot in the form of a bee with mechanical wings. It was purchased especially for First Lady Mamie Eisenhower.*

*Conrad N. Hilton, world-famous host, at the opening of his Beverly Hilton Hotel in California. It was the first luxury hotel to be built after World War II.*

But Eva Gabor was another matter. Erik, a union member now who could deliver food personally, arrived at her door with a snack tray she'd ordered. Glancing around, he asked her where she'd like him to put it. She gave him a once-over. Apparently she liked what she saw.

With her devilishly sexy Hungarian accent, she asked, "Do you come with that, darling?"

Erik could find no words to maneuver past his blush.

# Chapter Five
## But Where Is Houston?

*I was promoted to manager of the Steakhouse at the Statler Hilton in Los Angeles. After several months of a very successful operation, I was recommended for the catering director position at the Shamrock Hilton in Houston.*

Erik Worscheh likes to believe everything happens for a reason. If his crippled minesweeper hadn't drifted into a sandbar back in World War II, he might have fallen into Russian hands and perished in Siberia. If he hadn't accepted Margit's invitation to come to America, he might not have forged a career in hotel food and beverage management.

Fine. But back in 1958, he loved Beverly Hills, so what was the purpose of this latest distressful development, driving through dark rain and being lost on Houston's then-dismal Washington Avenue?

In Los Angeles, Erik had been promoted from his position at the Beverly Hilton to manager of the Statler Hilton's Steakhouse because the place needed a major infusion of creativity. He gave it his all, including a wash of pink lighting to flatter all the ladies. He knocked out a wall to expose the broiler station—customers could see the broiler chef in action and enjoy the aroma of close-up grilling. For tableside drama, a waiter rolled forth a gueridon so that diners might watch a classic Caesar salad created from scratch, or observe their Chateaubriand double thick or New York sirloin undergo precision slicing. Erik donned his finery and greeted guests at the door. [That sartorial devotion came from his days at the academy in Prague where it was normal for 15-years-olds to arrive at school with gloves and stylish walking canes. The memory amuses him now. "We were a little snobbish."]

Erik's innovations at the steakhouse brought a dramatic turn-around, from a dwindling clientele to triple the hotel's expectation for lunch and dinner. People lined up at the steakhouse door while the hotel's refined dining room experienced a decline in business.

With that success came another opportunity, this time to perform his magic at the latest Hilton acquisition. It was the Shamrock Hotel, built by oil tycoon Glenn McCarthy in his gusher heyday. Its eighteen stories and its elegant Emerald Ballroom and famous International Club (Continental Room) stood out in "nowhere," three miles from downtown Houston when much of

*His new job at the Shamrock Hilton presented Erik Worscheh with a Texas-sized opportunity to exercise his talents.*

the Texas Medical Center was still on paper. So immense was the Shamrock swimming pool, it could accommodate water skiing, and that fact rather summed up the Irish-themed flamboyance of the entire place. At its riotous, boozy opening, hundreds of Hollywood stars and notables from around the

*When the Shamrock Hilton was in full swing in the early '60s, a luau for 2200 guests featured splashy entertainment, including a floating orchestra in its Olympic-sized swimming pool.*

country attended a million dollar party, an astounding figure at that time. Crazy, vulgar, wild, fun-loving Texans managed to create national headlines and a long-lasting publicity hangover.

Then in 1952 wildcatter McCarthy hit a financial snag and gave up the property to the Equitable Life Assurance Society. The Hilton Hotels Corp. eventually moved in.

When the idea of transfer was broached to Erik by phone, he asked: "Where is Houston?"

The Statler Hilton manager, John Meacham, overheard one of Erik's conversations with Bob Leroy, director of Food and Beverage at the Shamrock. If he accepted, coaxed Leroy, Erik's title would be director of banquet sales, a move up in prestige and salary.

"Oh, no, stay with us," said Meacham when Erik hung up the phone. "It's so hot there, your pants will stick to your legs. Houston has nothing but rain and mosquitoes this big!" He indicated something the size of a tennis ball.

But Erik did accept, and now he agonized as he navigated Washington Avenue. Why hadn't he listened to Meacham's sterling advice? His car splashed forward through the gloom past nondescript buildings. Finally he found Main Street. He drove on, peering through a slapping windshield wiper. Dwellings became sparse—surely he had passed the Shamrock. So he turned. Bad move. His front wheels jumped a curb and lodged in spongy ground on an esplanade.

The cliché, "If he didn't have bad luck, he wouldn't have any luck at all" applied to Erik's early experiences with automobiles. In Riverside, he'd bought a used car from a Mission Inn employee for $28 (yes, twenty-eight dollars). Because he noticed that Southern California drivers never rolled their windows up in those pre-air conditioning days, he thought it natural that all this car's windows were down—until he discovered it had no window panes. At one point in Riverside, when driving the car home to show Margit, his foot went through the floorboard. Her reaction was the final insult: she would not allow such a calamity to be parked in front of her house. Erik dutifully traded the lesser machine in for a brown Hudson convertible which moved forward sensibly. Then he discovered it couldn't go in reverse. Repairs were expensive. Erik finally realized he had been naïve in assuming that the people he dealt with were honest. The next time he bought a car, he sought out a reputable dealer and a nice Buick—the one which now dug into Houston mud and refused to budge either backward or forward.

He had no choice other than leaving the car and all his possessions. He flagged down a motorist who explained that the hotel was farther out—he should have kept going. The man took pity on the distraught fellow with an accent and gave him a ride.

Erik dripped into the hotel lobby at ten p.m. The night manager, on hearing him claim to be the new director of catering, asked, "Where are your papers?" Erik explained they were stuck in the mud. The man promptly called a security officer and said, "We have a kook out here." Only after much persuasion did Erik get the belligerent officer to call up Bob Leroy, who had been waiting anxiously for Erik to arrive. The last time he'd talked to him on the phone, Erik was in San Antonio and, unacquainted with Texas distances, had promised to be in Houston in an hour or so.

"Send him up to the Presidential Suite," Leroy said, sounding much relieved and pleased. Abruptly a miserable night glowed warm with a bottle of champagne, canapés and a welcoming party. In no time, Erik's car and possessions got rescued under direction of a suddenly polite security guard.

\* \* \*

New York City's Waldorf-Astoria had its Oscar and Houston's Shamrock Hilton had its Erik. Often the public confused Oscar Tschirky's title, maitre d'hotel, with "head chef." He once explained that he didn't cook—scrambled eggs, maybe, but little else, since his wife wouldn't allow him in the kitchen. Instead, his job was twofold: first, coordinating the hotel staff behind the scenes, and second, working in front with a goal of fulfilling the public's every wish. Through well-trained assistants, Oscar's influence reached vast distances. One of his polished assistants, Fred Hayman, moved to the Beverly Hilton where he eventually became the guru of catering in Beverly Hills. In time he also became boss and mentor of young Erik Worscheh.

Erik, who seemed to have inherited his Mutti's stamina and strong work ethic, couldn't resist taking calls after the banquet office closed, which meant he often booked important parties. He enjoyed the sense of responsibility. Before long he offered to work in Hayman's office into the night without pay—that's how inspired he was by the Waldorf banquet system. The eventual result of his ambition was assignment to captain the head table for major functions, such as the Friar Club's madcap roasts hosted by movie and TV star Dean Martin. Erik got paid for these stints, but not for his routine volunteer duties in Hayman's banquet office. When Erik dared to mention extra salary, Hayman's response was, "Hey! You should have to pay me!" He wasn't joking. But he did give him the title of assistant, and as such, Erik immediately gained new status and recognition by the entire hotel staff. (Hayman later opened Georgio's on Rodeo Drive.)

Oscar's heyday occurred when New York society dared move its events from the salons of private mansions into public hotels. The idea was scandalous, but it caught on, especially after new-fangled automobiles and electricity forever changed the scene.

Decades later, Houston, which an early newspaper columnist labeled "a whiskey and trombone town," took New York City's idea to an extreme. It welcomed a hotel purposely designed for entertainment. Houston was expanding and wanted to be noticed. "Big" was good, but only "biggest" could satisfy a Texas standard. Now what the Shamrock also wanted under the Hilton auspices was an aura of class, a la Oscar.

Along came Erik in 1958, hired as catering manager.

And immediately along came the boisterous Houston Rodeo and Fat Stock Show. Genteel behavior would have to hold up in the pen.

Houston simply can't help it. Once a year, it has to honor its distant cowtown past, its horse trailers swaying on the freeways, its clattering covered wagon parade, its boots and saddle mentality. The reason for all this madness: the springtime show with all its eager volunteer workers brings BIG MONEY to a youth scholarship program—for instance, $8.4 million in 2007.

Erik sized up the Go-Texan party situation. He'd retire his preferred tuxedo temporarily and substitute a spiffy western-cut jacket and bolo tie, no matter that he'd never ridden a horse in his life. He'd confer with the chef to devise a traditional western menu—barbecued ribs and all the expected trimmings, and décor to match. His maxim, a tried and proven hand-me-down from Oscar of the Waldorf, was "give them what they want."

After that, what Shamrock-goers wanted was Erik Worscheh. Back in his formal attire, he orchestrated one resplendent presentation after another for thousands of formal balls and parties in the Emerald Room, the Grand Ballroom and International Club. These included major functions honoring state and national figures such as President Lyndon Johnson, Governor John Connally, Senator Lloyd Bentsen, Senator Barry Goldwater and Henry Kissinger.

Each year the Allegro Ball, lavishly decorated by the late esteemed interior designer, Edward J. Perrault, FASID, introduced a new crop of debutantes. After the socialites finished school, they reappeared for wedding celebrations. Cakes stretched ever higher. Erik's scrapbook contains a photo of one soaring confection whose majestic columns separate eight layers. Society columnists filled their space with accounts of the Grand Opera Ball, the Museum of Fine Arts gala, the Consular Ball, and political, civic and charity events galore.

Outside around that massive pool, Erik turned Hawaiian luaus into constant action—motor boats roaring, water skis spraying, and a group called the Corkettes famous for synchronized swimming. Hundreds of guests inhaled the heady bouquet of leis while they downed tropical drinks and feasted on island delicacies.

One day, as Erik watched the Corkettes' water ballet, he got an idea. He would ask the wait staff to perform synchronized table service. Thereafter, on a signal, gloved waiters surrounded each dinner table and with a flourish presented the main course to all guests simultaneously. The gustatory ballet

*Erik ordered gloves, wigs and Early American finery from Philadelphia's Opera House to outfit waiters who served an elaborate wedding reception at the Shamrock's Emerald Room*

could well have been set to music.

Desserts were never meek. Lights dimmed and the orchestra struck up a military tempo. Out of the kitchen marched a platoon of waiters with flaming swords and Baked Alaskas. The rousing act got applause every time; it became a Worscheh trademark to the delight of dignitaries and locals.

In those days, Texas laws forbade liquor by the drink except in private clubs. Membership in the Shamrock's International Club became a point of prestige and, for the hotel, a source of profit. The club wasn't merely a place to dine and drink—floor shows brought in a stream of headliners such as Robert Goulet, Judy Garland, the Mills Brothers, Wayne Newton, Carol

*In the early '60s at the Shamrock, this wedding cake made a striking display, being the tallest of its kind.*

Channing, Liza Minnelli and many other shining stars. Nightly, Shep Fields and his Rippling Rhythm Orchestra kept feet gliding about the dance floors. One memorable evening Mrs. Shep Fields invited Erik up to their suite for dinner, most of which she prepared, and the couple introduced him to their other guest, Tony Bennett.

Any place that invites celebrities also attracts the press. Walter Cronkite and Dan Rather, both originally from Houston, were frequent visitors; Rather set up shop there during Hurricane Carla. Local Houston Press gossip columnist Bill Roberts occupied the first table inside the door of the International Club. Later columnist Maxine Mesinger made it a morning routine to call Erik for news of the previous evening.

Erik, meanwhile, had become the Shamrock Hilton's food and beverage manager. His responsibilities included the International Club dining room and a new grand ballroom. To heighten his skills, he attended numerous training sessions around the country, thereby keeping up with the latest techniques in all the gradations of his domain. Charm and drama "up front" came naturally to Erik, but it was equally important to be ever mindful of revenue. On a grander scale, he learned to operate by "keeping the pencils sharp," according to Mutti's no-nonsense tradition of insuring profit.

He did this by establishing contacts, building new files and developing follow-up business across a broad spectrum of the community. The Shamrock Hilton became Houston's center of social, business and civic gatherings, as well as a mecca for national conventions.

*In the early '60s, Erik goes formal (as usual) for the Shamrock Hilton's first society gala.*

\* \* \*

One of Conrad Hilton's sons shared Erik's first name, but spelled it differently. It was a joke among hotel employees that when someone asked for either of the men, they should say, "Do you mean the rich one with a "c" or the poor one with the "k"?

As it turned out, the poor one with a "k" had some influence on the other, who came to the Shamrock in the '60s to contribute to the family empire by working in the sales department. His office was next to Erik's.

One day Erik's longtime friend, Dr. James Taylor of the University of Houston, made a polite but bold request. Would he mind asking Eric Hilton for a favor? Would Eric contact his father, the renowned Conrad Hilton, and ask for a donation to help create a hotel school?

Yes, he would and did, but Erik with the "k" got the feeling that Eric with the "c" was a bit hesitant. Perhaps he felt, as youngest of the three Hilton sons, that he didn't have a position of power in the family. His brothers Nicky and Barron (grandfather of the infamous Paris Hilton,) already had considerable business experience.

So for added insurance, Erik called Olive Wakeman, Conrad Hilton's administrative secretary. Not a bad idea, she said, because he likes Texas. He acquired his first hotel in Cisco, Texas. "But let's wait until he's in a good mood," she said. "That would be when he gets a statement with a favorable bottom line."

A few days later she called in great excitement. "Get Eric on the phone. I want to tell him to call his Dad."

Erik rushed to locate him. "Eric," he said, "call Olive Wakeman right now. Your Dad is in a good mood!"

In October, 1969, a special dinner at the Shamrock to honor Conrad Hilton himself culminated with a presentation—a personal check for $1,500,000. Thus was born the Conrad N. Hilton College of Hotel and Restaurant Management, which in 1983 received a grant of $21,350,000 from the Hilton Foundation to build a hotel tower on the University of Houston campus. Today the mid-campus site includes a full-service seven-floor Hilton hotel.

Erik served on the hotel school's

*Erik at one of the first lavish dinners of Les Amis d'Escoffier, held at the Houston Club.*

advisory council. He influenced decisions on kitchen design for banquet service and the student kitchen labs. In turn, he always made a point to help students rack up real-life banquet experience. He enabled them to work during private parties at Erik's various stations of employment. Several times he was invited to give classroom lectures.

In 2005, Erik was made an honorary alumnus of the Conrad N. Hilton College and in 2006 he received an honor that, in his opinion, summarized his professional achievements. He had served The Worrell Design Corp., a commercial kitchen design firm, as a consultant, and at a special dinner, its president, Rodney Worrell, presented a scholarship endowment to the college in the name of Erik J. Worscheh.

And the honors go on. In progress now is one that started with a chance encounter in the Memorial Hermann Hospital Restaurant where the Worschehs happened upon Dr. Richard S. Ruiz, one of the founders of the Hermann Eye Center.

Years before, ophthalmologists Dr. Ruiz and Dr. Whitney Sampson decided to form a Physicians' Food and Wine Society. To plan their kick-off dinner with all the appropriate ingredients, they were advised to call on Erik Worscheh at the Shamrock Hilton. Erik agreed to help. As expected, the event was a huge success, so much so that in ensuing years Dr. Ruiz expanded his interest to other food and wine societies. Along the way he noted the Worscheh influence in Houston's trend toward refinement in food, beverage and service.

When they met by chance, it took only minutes to rekindle their memories of that first dinner. Their animated talk brought Dr. Ruiz to a decision: The Worscheh contributions to Houston must be recognized. Back in his office, he picked up the telephone and began a campaign with the help of Dr. John Bowen, Dean, and Jon Schultz, Director of Development, to create a permanent visiting faculty endowment at the University of Houston's Conrad N. Hilton College of Hotel and Restaurant Management. During this period, Cathleen Baird, archivist of the college, conducted an oral interview with Erik and Mary. Listening in was enthusiastic Nick Massad, college alum and president of American Liberty Hospitality, Inc. The resulting question-and-answer session, rich with anecdotes and history, is now in of the school's permanent records.

Named for Erik Worscheh, the endowment continues to accept contributions. It has reached a goal set by the Conrad N. Hilton Foundation wherein the foundation will now match such contributions dollar-for-dollar.

# Chapter Six
## If It Isn't Loretta Young, Who Is It?

*I*n *April, 1958, a charming lady who was a buyer of handbags and small leather goods at Foley's appeared in my office to plan a Christmas party for Foley's Executive Club. She had a very low budget of $5 per person.*

If the Shamrock stood as a sentinel toward the south of the city, then a department store dominated downtown Houston, not in height but by impact. In those pre-tunnel days, Main Street's sidewalks were shoulder-to-shoulder crowded and rare was the dedicated shopper who didn't stop at Foley's for lunch in the Azalea Terrace and a bit of impulse charging.

One of Foley's professional buyers, however, had a mission at the Shamrock. Tall, attractive Mary Boney, elected to plan and implement the executives' Christmas party, decided it was time to switch from the aged Rice Hotel setting to a place more sophisticated. Armed with her Rice Hotel party menu, she asked to see the Shamrock's catering manager. Soon she faced Erik Worscheh. With his foreign accent and ready smile, he was all charm, she thought. But his brows furrowed when she named the price she'd pay—only five dollars per person for a full dinner, including dessert, tax, tips and set-ups. (Texas law forbade serving liquor but allowed certain establishments to bring out glasses, ice and soda, etc., to mix with alcohol that patrons brought discreetly from home). The price Mary quoted had always been so, and she wasn't about to change.

"But, this *is* the Shamrock," Erik protested.

Her eyes flashed determination. Was he a newcomer? If so, she'd need to enlighten him. She explained that Foley's was the most prestigious store in Houston and hosting the party would be to the Shamrock Hilton's infinite advantage. The newer hotel would be exposed to executives of vast influence, she insisted.

It wasn't so much that the Shamrock needed prestige and connections beyond what notables such as queens and presidents and stars had already provided. What mattered to Erik at the moment was that this feisty young Mary looked like Loretta Young, one of his favorite stars.

Mary tried another approach. Noting his accent, she asked him where he originated. That led to a discussion about Europe and her recent business trips abroad. Erik marveled at her knowledge and that one so young would have the responsibility of a buying trip every year to London, Paris, Florence, Brussels and Frankfurt.

The Shamrock might consider her request, he told her, but he'd have to talk it over with the chef and would let her know in three days. (Much later he confessed he had the authority to make that decision immediately and independently.)

He called her three days later, and yes, five dollars would be workable because of Foley's importance to the community. That would even include tips and set-ups. Again, it was the tenet of the Waldorf's Oscar: give them what they want!

But Erik wanted something more. He was interested in seeing Mary again. If he ever got downtown, he told her, he'd stop in and buy her a cup of coffee.

He never did, although he might have made a greater effort had he known that Mary told her sister, Melba, with whom she shared an apartment, that she'd met an interesting man, and wondered aloud if he was married. Pressing duties for both in the next few months precluded further thought of meeting. Then Mary showed up at the Shamrock in September and again in October to settle party arrangements.

It pleased Erik to escort her on a tour of the facilities. This time the flame of romance lighted and did not flicker out.

After their meeting, Erik suggested that they have a drink away from the hotel. Mary agreed. How about her nearby apartment? He could follow her in his car. Good, he said.

But after driving several blocks, Mary suddenly regretted her action—she had invited a strange man to her apartment, moreover a foreigner. Her two trips abroad had left her suspicious of European men who, whether married or not, had proved entirely too forward around defenseless American girls. On the other hand, she worried that Erik might be thinking she was a pickup.

Not exactly. It was Erik who was anxious. From Mary's indication that her apartment was "nearby," he pictured it to be two or three blocks from the hotel. He'd been following her for several miles and puzzled over where she could be leading him.

When they finally pulled up to Mary's apartment, she was mightily relieved to find her sister and sister-in-law at home. "I felt much more at ease," she said.

Conversation flowed naturally. The evening went so well that Erik, who turned out to be a gentleman, asked her for a later dinner date, and she was pleased to accept.

However, their serious courtship began with some embarrassment on Erik's part. Because he always had his meals at the Shamrock, he never carried money, a fact he overlooked the evening he took Mary to the then-popular Bud Bigelow's steakhouse. These were pre-credit card days. When the check came, he suffered the chagrin of having to ask her to pass him cash under the table.

By late fall these two ambitious people found a lasting personality kinship. Erik was impressed that Mary's work ethic appeared as motivated as his own. With a degree from Baylor University, she had come to Houston in 1949 after accepting a job with Foley's on its executive training program. She progressed to assistant manager in linens, then women's ready-to-wear, and became buyer and department manager of handbags, small leather goods and belts in 1953 at the age of 23. She made buying trips to New York City four to five times each year during a period of ten years. In 1956, she made her first European trip and each spring for the next seven years, traveled in Europe.

Although Mary's background lacked the tensions of Erik's minesweeping and emigration, it provided bedrock for career-building. Her father, a resolute man who left home to work at age thirteen and saved enough money to put himself through Toby Business School in Waco, instilled in Mary the kind of discipline that catapulted her into merchandising.

Mary was born on Aug. 4, 1929, long after W.A. (Arthur) Boney (1885-1967) married Susan Lena Stewart (1890-1961) and moved to Iola, Texas. She was the seventh of their eight children. Her enterprising father had become president of the Iola State Bank. In 1919 he formed the Farmers Gin Co., which consisted of two cotton gins, and thereby became a cotton broker. Later he opened Boney Bros. General Merchandise Store and also the Boney Insurance Agency, a lumber yard and bought a ranch for raising Hereford cattle.

*Arthur and Lena Boney, parents of Mary Worscheh, as they posed for their wedding picture.*

In order of birth, the Boney children were W. A. Jr., who became a veterinarian, Stewart, CPA; Harold, who died in an auto accident while a freshman at the University of Texas; Frances Slaughter, secretary/accountant; John, cost accountant; Melba Wells, medical technologist; Mary, and Dixie DuBose, realtor-broker. Only Mary, Frances and Melba sur-

*Melba, Dixie and Mary Boney, left to right, enjoyed sisterly closeness in Iola, Texas.*

vive. As with many large families, lives diverged over the years. But Mary is particularly grateful for the bittersweet time spent with her beloved "Baby Sister" Dixie, who often stayed with the Worschehs while undergoing treatments at M. D. Anderson Hospital.

Mary admired her mother's take-charge attitude during the Great Depression. Lena ran the store's dry goods department and did all the bookkeeping. She bought and sold merchandise and assisted locals with work clothes, fabrics and sewing accessories. It fascinated Mary to watch her mother cut an odd measurement, say one and two-thirds yards, then quickly calculate the price in her head.

If Arthur thought his wife was more into buying than selling, they'd have a serious "discussion," during which he tried to teach her the need for a careful budget. Even so, both parents made allowances for hard times. Neither could resist donating food and clothing to the needy or permitting a debt to ride. At the store and at the bank, Arthur showed deep respect for local farmers and cattlemen who were desperate victims of the times. He gave them the loans they needed until crops came in, and he suggested they pay the bank debts first in order to uplift the local economy, and pay the store whenev-

*Mary's formal wedding portrait by Gittings.*

er they could. "Don't worry about it," he'd say. He knew them all and cherished them as friends and customers.

Meanwhile, Arthur expected his children to do their share of work in the store, particularly on Saturdays. Mary's earliest job was behind the candy counter. When her father saw her distracted by chatty friends, he took her aside and said, "You can't stand and talk to your friends. The customer won't want to bother you." One day when she experienced a lull, she decided to sit on a tall stool and read comic books. Her father again disapproved—an approaching customer might not want to disturb her, he said. These lessons stayed with Mary. As an adult at a Foley's weekly training meeting, she cautioned the salespeople not to "gang up" at the register and chat, making customers feel unwelcome.

It was her understanding of the business world (besides looking like Loretta Young) that impressed Erik. He proposed the following fall.

Then he suggested they get married the day after Christmas, the least hectic time in the hotel business. In her excitement, Mary agreed, forgetting entirely that the very same day is the year's most feverish for any department store—traditionally, that's when all the gift returns pour in. Foley's buyers, acting as department managers, were expected to be on duty, report to their floors, meet the public and expedite customer needs. There were few excuses—except maybe a wedding.

*The day after Christmas in 1959 was a day to remember all their lives. Mary Boney from a little Texas town became the bride of Erik Worscheh, a persuasive fellow with a German-Bohemian accent.*

*Mary's parents, Arthur and Lena Boney, Baptists, at their daughter's Catholic wedding.*

Erik and Mary were married on Dec. 26, 1959, at St. Vincent's Catholic Church, five minutes from the Shamrock Hilton. It's doubtful that her fellow employees complained about her absence from duty because among the wedding guests was Max Levine, president of Foley's. Also in attendance were Erik's sister Margit, her husband Jimmy and their four children, Jonathan, Jennifer, Jessica and Jeffrey, who had traveled from Georgia for the ceremony. They arrived in time to celebrate Christmas at the Shamrock Hilton.

In those days the Catholic Church decreed that a non-member take marriage vows at the railing instead of the altar. Mary was a Baptist and accepted the restriction with grace, but Erik wanted drama. He talked the priest into allowing the center aisle to be defined by a white runner, thereby giving his bride more of a theatrical approach. Jimmy was his best man and Betty Viau, Mary's roommate and fellow buyer at Foley's, was maid of honor.

As she floated down the aisle, the bride glimpsed most of her large Baptist family. They all looked a bit awed because it was their first time to set foot in a Catholic Church.

In 1961, after accompanying Erik to many a Mass, she decided to take instructions in the

*Newlyweds Erik and Mary expected and got a long, happy life together.*

evenings after work at the near-by Annunciation Catholic Church. She was baptized on August 30 that year. The joy of Erik and Mary's wedding day was equaled only by the birth of their son, Mark, in 1963, and later echoed by his accomplish-ments.

*Mary Worscheh in 1960.*

\* \* \*

Not long after their wedding and honeymoon in Mexico City, Mary learned that marriage to a hotel man was somewhat of a mirage. Her husband left the house by eight in the morning and didn't show up again until ten or eleven at night. On his days off, they almost had to get reacquainted.

"You have to create a life of your own," she said. She learned to make the most of free weekends or the business trip where spouses are welcome. She stayed on at Foley's for a few years until Mark was born. Erik's long hours at work left her with child-rearing duties much like those of a single mother. Cub scouts, school events, summer plans—all of it kept Mary in a happy whirlwind until she realized that while Mark was in school, she could keep the same hours in gainful employ-ment. Through the influence of Edith Patterson, a friend from Baylor Days who was a teacher at Bellaire High School, Mary again signed on in the workaday world. She took a job teach-ing distributive education (now called marketing education) at Lee High School, and later at Lamar.

In 1969 Mary returned to Foley's as divisional sales man-ager, fashions, of the Almeda store. In 1973, she tried some-thing new. She earned a license and joined Madeleine O'Brien Realtors to become a broker in residential real estate. Just when she reached a point of retirement, literally a higher calling had her accepting management of Bayou Bend Towers, a twenty-three story luxury condominium. Mary's new career brought an extra reward for the Worschehs, a lasting friendship with her accomplished assistant, Norma Coogan, and her husband, Fred.

In 1995 Mary finally gave herself permission to slow the pace. She turned to satisfying volunteer work and to an impressive amount of travel with Erik.

Their most unusual trip had to be the jaunt involving one of Houston's novel characters, a man with the heart of a showman and the wild impulses to make things happen on demand. The journey is described in Chapter Eight.

And despite their scant daytime togetherness, Mary and Erik's marriage evolved into the kind where they finish each other's sentences, where Mary wants him along on a fashion shopping trip because she respects his judgment of her try-ons, where they both cherish their highly organized collections of books, scrapbooks, framed pictures and mementoes. Under Erik's influence, she became well versed in the matter of fine food and elegant entertaining. And under her guidance, Erik slowly adopted Texas ways. Mary notes that his only deficiency—sort of a character flaw in Texas—is that he adamantly refuses to wear jeans.

# Chapter Seven
## Carrying on the Name

*T*he birth of Mark in 1963 brought new excitement into the already full lives of Erik and Mary Worscheh. They delighted in their child's development. Early on, it seemed he would possess unrestrained curiosity and an eagerness to learn. Unfortunately, Erik's job kept him working far into most nights, so he missed a lot of Mark's waking childhood. On the other hand, those times he could share often turned into amazing advantages for the youngster.

*And then there were three. Mary and Erik with little Mark Erik on the day of his baptism.*

When Erik needed to attend a conference or visit relatives, he took his wife and son along. Their trips included Hawaii, Vancouver, the wine regions of France, along with other countries in Europe and major cities of the U.S. Mark became an eager world traveler before he even entered school.

When he was two, he met his grandmother "Omi" for the first time—this was Mutti, then staying with Margit and Jim in Madrid. She was proud to take him along to a small cathedral across the street. He didn't know the prayers, but the life-sized crucifix at the front of the church caught his attention. He approached the bare feet of Jesus, touched each toe and began reciting in some volume, "This Little Piggy Went to Market." Mutti's alarmed shushing him made little difference and soon the entire congregation was laughing.

The alphabet and numbers were pre-school accomplish-

*Mary and Erik with cheerful baby Mark, age 18 months.*

ments, forerunners of topnotch grades throughout school. He had principles, too, Mary recalls. Each morning as he left for a short walk to school, he'd first look up and down the street to see if anyone was looking before he let his mother kiss him good-bye.

In the interest of a fulfilling family life, the Worschehs bought a home in Meyerland, about five minutes from the Shamrock. The neighborhood brimmed with congenial adults and active children. The short commute gave Erik a tad more time with Mark and Mary and more new friends to cherish—Chuck and Sam Caruso, for instance, who lived across the street and helped celebrate many a family and holiday gath-ering. Mark wasted no time find-ing friends either, helped no doubt by the lures of a ping-pong table and a swimming pool with shower at the Worscheh residence One kind neighbor built a special gate in his back yard so that children on the block could cut through his property for a handier route to Lovett Elementary School.

*Mark and his Dad enjoy some infrequent but cherished time together.*

A Worscheh party attraction was a lanai covered with about 200 grass skirts. Overhead, a 1905 Westinghouse ceiling fan shuffled the night air. On many a festive weekend Mark acted as waiter, imitating the discreet presence of the servers he had observed in hotel set-tings. At the tender age of nine, he did such duty around the pool when the Worschehs entertained Judge Roy Hofheinz and about forty others with a rollicking luau. The adults settled with their food on one side of the pool, but Mark lounged alone in a chair across the water. His father called to him, urging him to join the group. But young Mark declined.

To their amusement, he answered eloquently: "I'm perfectly content. I have my good food, I have my aged drink (a Coke bottle wrapped in a napkin as if it were wine)—and I have the moon."

Erik made up for paternal absenteeism by buying a home on a Texas lake, where he and Mark took on the roles of premier fishermen. Once they perfected the technique, they advanced to the big-time cold streams of mountainous New Mexico and Colorado. Those adventures came in the summers when the Worschehs rented a motor home. The first year Erik drove the massive machine off in a burst of confidence, but soon had to stop at a station and,

*Mark, age 7, traveled extensively with his parents. Shown here with his mother at a historic wine cellar in the Burgundy region of France, he holds a rare 1911 bottle of Romanée-Conti.*

swallowing his pride, get someone to explain the function of all the buttons on the dash and of other mysterious knobs throughout. One summer they drove in tandem with friends Dick and Dianne Bynum and daughter Kathryn, also in a rental vehicle, and stopped at scenic camp sites where they fished for dinner. Erik named himself Chef de Cuisine, master of grilling and cooking, but his diners complained because the food seemed to take forever to cook. Erik finally learned that mountain air with its thinner oxygen requires different rules for food preparation—if he didn't want to hear wails of

*Mark Worscheh, age 18.*

hunger, he'd have to start the fire earlier.

A natural follow-up for Mark's water experiences was life-guarding at the Shamrock Hilton. After all, it seemed like another home—the youngster and Mary ate many a meal at the Charcoal Terrace, one of Erik's domains.

Mark was active in Boy Scouts, although when he reached his teens, he didn't publicize the fact around school. Scouting wasn't "cool" at the time, not nearly as desirable as his football playing or working on the school paper, or even acting in school plays at St. John's. He eventually achieved his Eagle Scout award, and with the help of fellow scouts, completed his project of building playground equipment for Lovett Elementary School.

His zenith of "coolness" occurred when he acquired his dream car, a Cougar, which a garage man diagnosed as "needing a little work." Mark proceeded to personally replace every part, including the radiator and the interior lining.

Mark graduated with honors and went on to Notre Dame, where he became managing editor of the college paper. He graduated cum laude. His degree in finance and economics impressed the New York investment bank Salomon Brothers, so he got a taste of living in the Big Apple. Two years later he earned his MBA at Stanford University on the opposite side of the country. Because he was always reluctant to reveal his own accomplishments, his parents had to learn about the scholastic honors on their own. "He never mentioned them," said Erik.

Merrill Lynch hired Mark as a corporate finance associate. While in training, he met Sue Mullen, a very attractive and intelligent fellow trainee from Britain, who had earned an MBA at INSEAD, one of the world's leading graduate business schools, located in Fontainebleau, France. Sue's father was a colonel and attaché to the Royal Air Force. He and wife, Virginia, and children, Sue and Nigel, had lived in various countries of the Commonwealth. Sue and Mark dated for a time

*Newlyweds Mark and Sue Worscheh with Erik and Mary at St. Clement Danes Church in London.*

until Sue was transferred back to London. Then the transatlantic romance began, progressing to a fairytale wedding on September 26, 1992.

For their rites, Mark and Sue chose the historic St. Clement Danes Church on the Strand, the Church of the Royal Air Force in London. It was originally built in the 1400s, but was decimated several times during various wars. It was rebuilt after World War II with donations from countries around the world. The U.S. Air Force contributed the organ and the Worschehs still talk about its magnificent music and how acoustics favored the choir in the balcony with breathtaking sounds.

British women attending the wedding were easily distinguished by their beautiful hats. Only an occasional American woman was so adorned. The difference was obvious by the fact that the bride's guests seated as a group on one side created a sea of hats and on the other, the American guests displayed mainly a mass of admirable hair-dos. Mary recalls that

*Worscheb children, with backpacks*

her biggest problem in preparing for the occasion was finding a hat in Houston—she finally borrowed a vintage model from a friend.

Approximately 60 American friends and relatives, from California to New York, attended the wedding. Mark's best man and long-time friend, Jeff Walters, traveled from Texas along with his parents, Jeanette and King Walters. The reception began nearby in the courtyard of the Inns of Court and was followed by a seated dinner in the historic and majestic Middle Temple. It was here that Mary spotted another cultural difference: the British ladies stopped in the foyer to deposit their hats on a long table.

Mark and Sue now live in Houston. Mark is Executive Vice President of Aquinas Corporation, a privately held national real estate and construction management firm and parent company of Linbeck Group and other related companies. Their three lovely-and-lively daughters, Hannah, Sophie and Amy, are students at St. John's School.

*Mark, Sue and girls at castle in Scotland*

*Everybody smile! It's a close-knit family of Worschehs: Mark and Sue, Mary and Erik and the granddaughters, Amy (center), and in foreground, left, Hannah, and right, Sophie. The occasion was a luncheon celebrating Erik's 80th birthday, memorable for yet another event—it snowed that day!*

# Chapter Eight
## A Circus Looking for a Circus

*I* *move to Astroworld Hotel Complex at request of Judge Roy Hofheinz and general manager Jim Spring. The National Homebuilders Association had plans to hold its convention in Houston. Members needed a ballroom to seat 2,200 people.—EJW*

"Erik, do you have a passport?"

"Yes."

"Does Mary have a passport?"

"Yes. Why do you ask?"

Judge Roy Hofheinz explained. He wanted to take a few friends to Europe to spot some circus acts. He'd need Erik to commandeer the dining along the way. The trip would last three weeks or so.

In a sense, the conversation on that day epitomized Erik Worscheh's collection of amazements from 1969-1973. He'd been lured away from the Shamrock by Judge Hofheinz, Houston's ex-mayor who poured his considerable energy and money into building an empire. It included the Domed Stadium (Eighth Wonder of the World, no less) and the Astroworld Hotel Complex, one of its hotels boasting the $2,500-per-night Celestial Suite. (Elvis Presley slept there.) National fanfare kept Houston and the Judge in the mood to keep on super-building, and soon plans materialized for a ballroom to accommodate the National Home Builder's Association, which would be the largest professional group ever assembled in Houston.

Having met Erik on numerous occasions at the Shamrock, Judge Hofheinz knew he'd spotted the man to coordinate and specify the ballroom needs, especially behind-the-scenes work stations. Erik, with the help of kitchen designers, could estimate how many ovens, grills, refrigerators, pots, dishes and personnel it would take to create smooth and memorable feasts. For certain, he had the know-how to execute a dinner of this expected magnitude.

When the invitation came from the Judge's general manager, Jim Spring, Erik reacted boldly from his position of strength at the Shamrock. He'd agree to join the Judge's operation, he said, but only if he could be named assistant general manager of food and beverage operations. There was no point moving, he figured, if the job wasn't a step up. The surprising response from Spring was, "Call yourself anything you like! Just come along."

The Shamrock had seemed large enough, but the Astro Village was like a city unto itself. Erik realized he'd be dealing with four hotels and exclusive sky boxes in the immense domed stadium, which had debuted three years earlier. It was a challenge he couldn't resist. He signed on.

Carpenters completed the grand ballroom structure on deadline. However, with 2,200 visitors only hours from convening, it lacked finishing touches. Rolls of carpet still stood upright. Some kitchen appliances weren't in place. The maitre d' gave in to a case of nerves. Most foreboding, the menu for the evening promised *Tournedos Rossini* topped with *foie gras* for each guest and the broilers were not functional. Erik quickly directed the chef to use a bank of portable ovens (Carter Hofmanns). Hours ahead, the meats were marked with grill lines—branded, in kitchen parlance—and placed in the ovens at low heat over Sterno. Chef Gunter Lowe's timing worked. To Erik's relief, the steaks exemplified perfection, moist and tender as butter.

Even so, the unexpected was not excluded. Erik's now-famous flaming swords and Baked Alaska dessert routine hit a snag. Lights dimmed. The orchestra struck up a fanfare and military beat. High-stepping waiters emerged from the kitchen with blazing swords held aloft in full drama. But just as they entered the ballroom, they passed under an aggressive air-conditioning vent and one by one, the flames were blasted out, leaving the ballroom in the dark. Erik, armed with a new-fangled walkie-talkie, sent an urgent coded message to the lighting man. On cue, psychedelic red, blue and green light beams swept wildly around the room. Next, he signaled the orchestra leader: "Play the *Eyes of Texas!*" Texan or not, all the conventioneers responded by boisterous singing. Some even stood on their chairs and whirled napkins to the beat. When they recovered from the excitement, they found Baked Alaskas glistening on their plates.

Thus initiated, the huge ballroom joined the Celestial Suite to become a unique center of entertainment in the city. The multi-room suite was a talked-about attraction with its miniature electronic scoreboard replicating the Dome's extravaganza, and the Judge's remarkable collection of circus memorabilia, including weirdly-animated musical instruments that played without human assistance. His two-story Tarzan room nestled amid vines; the South Pacific hut featured mosquito netting over the bed; the main suite-within-a-suite featured a Roman bath, and so on throughout thirteen eye-boggling rooms. National publicity about the Judge's legendary digs used words and phrases as "spectacular," "sports fan's dream," and "testament to excess that dwarfs all competitors"—these descriptions from one column alone, by Stephen Birnbaum

What Erik remembers with perhaps the greatest pride are the Splashdown parties in the Celestial Suite for Houston's— America's—astronauts. The famous crew, Jim Lovell, Jack Swigert and Fred Haise, (since made extra-famous by Tom Hanks' suspenseful *Apollo 13* movie) were honored there. Another party celebrated the crew of Apollo 17, Jack Schmitt, Gene Cernan and Ron Evans. Erik has a bumper crop of astronaut autographs and photos paving one wall of his den. Its focal point is a large and rare photo of the moon landing. On the picture's white mat are the signatures of thirty-one original astronauts plus a notation of thanks to Erik for a great party.

Another luminary in space activity and exploration of the time was rocket scientist Wernher Von Braun. At several Astroworld Hotel functions in conjunction with NASA events, he apparently appreciated down-to-earth conversations with Erik.

*Erik and Mary stand on either side of NASA's Capt. James Lovell and wife Marilyn, guests at a celebration party in the Celestial Suite of the Astroworld Hotel.*

Judge Roy Hofheinz' enthusiasm for the Big Top reached a peak in 1967 when he and a couple of friends formed a holding company and bought the famous Ringling Bros. Circus. The Greatest Show on Earth divided into two shows for even greater reach, and as board chairman, the Judge saw a need for more eye-popping acts. That's when he decided to take a group of twenty-six besides himself and his wife, Mary Frances, to Europe. They would travel behind the communist block in search of talent. He gave his friends and their spouses, including Erik and Mary, scant notice,

*Captain James A. Lovell Jr, commander of Apollo 13 lunar mission in 1970.*

*Apollo 17 astronaut Captain Eugene A. (Gene) Cernan.*

only enough time to settle issues with employers, employees and baby sitters, to get needed shots, and to pack one suitcase per person. In contrast, the Judge, by then in a wheelchair because of a recent stroke, took 40 pieces of luggage.

At the Houston airport, the Judge handed Erik a wad of money, approximately ten thousand dollars. He was told to put it in his pocket and use it to pay overweight charges at various airports. The Judge's excess baggage included a gallon jar of Tabasco sauce. Special therapy equipment for his exercise routine necessitated a personal therapist and all-round attendant. Other key professionals besides Erik in the entourage were two nurses, two doctors and three lawyers. The rest were friends and business associates.

Some hours later, Sofia, Bulgaria, a city of approximately a million at the time, nearly went into shock. Theirs was a quiet little airport because few citizens were allowed to travel in those restricted days. Suddenly a Texas spectacle materialized, led by a man in a wheelchair. The epaulets of his military-type jacket flashed with unusual

*After Judge Roy Hofheinz took a large contingent of Texans to many parts of Europe in search of circus acts, the fun-filled trip was relived by his fellow travelers in the Celestial Suite.*

medals (Domed Stadium buttons). He wore a black sealskin hat, black horned-rimmed glasses and, with an authoritative air, smoked an outrageously long cigar.

No way could the sparse personnel handle all the luggage spilling out of the Texans' plane. Suspicious inspectors peered into a couple of suitcases, then gave up and allowed the baggage to line up outside until a rented truck could haul it off to the hotel of choice.

Despite language barriers and bewildered locals, the

*Mary and Erik at the Acropolis in Greece, one of the many stops on Judge Roy Hofheinz' fabulous search in Europe for circus acts.*

Astrogang took off running from one circus to another, from one country to the next, hitting the high spots in Budapest, Vienna, Athens, Lisbon, Frankfurt and Madrid.

Ah, Madrid—and ah, the Castellana Hilton. It would be the perfect place for a Spanish omelet, decided the Judge. He ordered one sent up to his room. When it arrived, he lifted the clear domed lid. What he saw plainly upset him. In his mind, the breakfast eggs should have been folded over a rich blend of tomatoes, parsley, onion, garlic and green pepper. He sent for his food specialist.

"Erik," he complained, "I asked for a Spanish omelet. This thing is just eggs and mushrooms. Where are the peppers, tomatoes and onions?"

Erik also raised the dome and peered at the presentation. "Well, Judge," he said analytically, careful to hide his amusement. "This *is* an omelet. And this *is* Spain."

The Judge would have none of it. He dispatched Erik to the kitchen to show the staff what a real Spanish omelet is supposed to look like. In Texas, anyway.

Throughout the trip, it was Erik's duty to see that mealtimes for the group went smoothly. In Budapest, after scouting the city, he arranged a five-course dinner with as many wines, along with strolling musicians. It cost $2.83 per person. In Athens, he set up a special dinner in the elegant dining room atop the Athens Hilton, and later another gathering at a small Greek restaurant. Festivities included dinner, a show and dancing.

Mary, like the other wives, enjoyed shopping, but perhaps the biggest buyer was the Judge himself. He and Mary Frances came home with thousands of dollars worth of elaborate merchandise and—the Judge's weakness—all sorts of historic military ribbons, medals and commemorative buttons. In their wake, hotel gift shops were left almost bare.

*Judge Roy Hofheinz hosted many a party in his Astroworld Hotel's whimsical Celestial Suite. Standing, left to right, Mary Frances Hofheinz, "Red" James, a former Hofheinz partner, and Mary and Erik Worscheh.*

The Worschehs cherish a special memory of that trip. Knowing Erik was close to his European family, the Judge gave him a bonus trip while the rest stayed behind. Erik and Mary boarded a train in Frankfurt for Ansbach and gave Mutti a huge surprise—she had no advance notice of the joyous two-day visit. At the time, she was residing in a nursing home. They also had the rare opportunity to visit Erik's cousin, Wolfgang Birk and his beautiful wife, Anne, in downtown Vienna. The Birks, who had been prominent in the Austrian movie industry, were delighted to entertain their American visitors.

The Judge had yet another brainstorm. In Athens, he leased a plane to accommodate the entire group, destination Salonika in northern Greece. He wanted to work a deal with the ranchers to buy and raise Texas cattle, thereby giving the "deprived" people of Athens an opportunity to put some top quality steaks on their platters. The deal never progressed beyond enthusiastic talk, but the Astrogang had a marvelous time at the ranch.

A few short weeks after their return to the U.S., the group reunited at the Celestial Suite. Erik's menu duplicated dishes they had relished in Sophia, Budapest, Athens and Vienna. Well-rested now, the guests insisted the menu was even tastier than the originals. They appeared in clothing or jewelry acquired on the trip and also brought baubles made of ersatz gold. At their request, the Judge's cabinet maker had constructed a giant scales. The Judge, again bedecked in military fashion with his splendid new collection of buttons, plus an imposing royal headdress, was asked to sit on one side of the scales while guests piled their fake metal on the other. The idea was to prove that their host was worth his weight in gold. He didn't quite fulfill the theory (perhaps he'd enjoyed too many of Erik's feasts, or to be kinder, it may have been the influence of all his medals), but his *joie de vivre* and energy kept his guests laughing and reminiscing into the night.

# Chapter Nine
## Going Up in the World—Really Up

*H*e'd worked for powerful, super-wealthy bosses before—Conrad Hilton, Judge Roy Hofheinz—but never so many all in one place.

In 1973, Erik's friend, Lynton (Uppy) Upshaw, confided that he would soon retire as long-time manager of the Petroleum Club of Houston. Erik should think about replacing him, he suggested.

But serious doubts rightly challenged such an offer. Erik had won considerable respect at the Astroworld Complex, and "complex" was a definitive description of his far-flung, ever-fascinating duties. The Judge trusted him to make the right decisions in most areas of the vast food and beverage operation. Wouldn't managing a private club be a come-down?

Uppy was positive that the Worscheh touch could do wonders at the prestigious downtown club and told its board so in glowing terms. Erik and Uppy had often worked together on The Petroleum Club's annual ball, after it moved to the larger Shamrock Emerald Room. Several years later the beautiful event "followed" Erik to the Astroworld Ballroom. Consequently, many of the oilmen already knew Erik from these contacts.

Uppy kept after him. As it turned out, timing was right. The Astroworld Complex purse was tightening. (Eventually the Judge relinquished ownership.) Erik's initial reluctance turned into a maybe and finally acceptance. He joined Uppy in an elevator ride up to the 43rd floor of the Exxon Building where the Petroleum Club sprawled. To look out of its windows was to view a grand sweep of downtown Houston and, with a little imagination, to envision the coastal terrain where Texas defines a stretch of the Gulf of Mexico.

Houston considered itself the oil capital of the world. No telling how many oil wells a full panorama of the area might include; even so, they would be only a small portion of the liquid gold represented by membership in this distinguished club. Its history, initiated late in 1951 in the Rice Hotel's top floor, included a series of strong-willed chairmen, officers, committees and directors, all accustomed to expressing themselves (from mild-mannered to hotheaded) and getting things done.

Given a project, appointed committees immediately drilled into research with the intention of making the best decision for the board and ultimately the membership. As manager of the club, Erik's experience and observations often became a necessary part of the research.

All this precise organization matched Erik's idea of how the world should turn, how day-to-day life should play out. It fit his orderly inclination that long ago enabled him to control a minesweeper in pitching icy waters, to mobilize scattered waiters at the Mission Inn, and more recently to translate a swim team's synchronization to impressive table service. Did he imagine that over his shoulder Mutti was nodding her head in approval?

But status quo wasn't enough. Once he delineated his area of responsibility and understood the precise pecking order, Erik formulated objectives for himself and the club. This, he vowed, would be the best club in America. Impeccable service, the finest food and flawless social events would be presented along with fiscal well-being and ideal working conditions for his staff.

Erik learned that employees needed an adequate health insurance plan and a retirement program. The kitchen staff needed restructuring. He made these necessities his goals. Party business wanted improvement. Erik opened that door by booking major culinary and social affairs which included classic dinners for *Les Amis d'Escoffier*, the *Confrerie des Chevaliers du Tastevin*, *Confrerie des Chaine des Rotisseurs*, the International Wine and Food Society and Bordeaux Society. There would be elegant wine tastings and seminars. Unfortunately, the club's collection of fine wines was housed in the only available space at the time, Exxon's basement. The inconvenience meant only a few cases of wine at a time could leave their chilly nest and rise to the service areas.

With Erik's encouragement, the Wine Committee stood firm in wanting a special cooled room upstairs. Its decor should be urbane; it would be not only a storage room but also a gathering place for connoisseurs. Erik, with knowledge of cellars from as far back as the family hotel in Czechoslovakia, pictured a fine hand-crafted wood table long enough to seat twenty-six people.

But several board members dawdled on this matter. The Wine Committee meanwhile had to put up with jocularities, such as hearing themselves referred to as "winos." Finally they took positive action and wooed the board with a knockout dinner and appropriate wines, a ploy which resulted in a more tractable attitude. The renovation was approved. Erik considered it a personal victory, as did the service staffers who no longer had to make those long, repeated elevator rides to the basement for supplies.

Perhaps the loftiest accomplishment, literally, of the Board of Directors was the agreement with Exxon to acquire the oil company's observation deck on the 45ᵗʰ floor. It had been closed to tourists and after remodeling, the considerable unused space proved perfect for the club's executive quarters and accounting office. Where those offices had been now welcomed a sophisticated wine cellar and private party rooms— Erik knew these to be money makers from his experience at the Beverly Hilton hotel.

The Petroleum Club of Houston became ever more pres-

# L'Escriteau

### L'Apertif

*Louis Roederer*
*Cristal, Brut*
*1975*

### Les Vins

*Schloss Johannisberger,*
*Auslese,*
*1976*

*Le Montrachet*
*Domaine Baron Thénard*
*1981*

*Château Petrus*
*1971*

*Château Mouton Rothschild*
*1961*

*Château Latour*
*en Jeroboam*
*1945*

*Boal Madeira*
*1863*

### La Reception

*Les Caviars de Beluga d'Iran*
*Sevruga de Russie et Osetra*
*Les Malossols Américaine*
*avec la Garniture Traditionnelle*
*La Mousse de Homard Bellevue*
*Les Poissons fumé*

### Le Diner

*LA PREMIERE ASSIETTE* — *La Caille farcie*

*LA DEUXIEME ASSIETTE* — *L'Extrait de Queue de Boeuf au Xérès*

*LA TROISIEME ASSIETTE* — *L'Escalope de Turbot Arlequin*

*LA QUATRIEME ASSIETTE* — *Le Rognon de Veau à la Garonne*

*POUR SE RAFRAICHIR* — *Le Sorbet de Kiwi*

*LA CINQUIEME ASSIETTE* — *Le Filet d'Agneau aux Herbes*
*Les Pommes Savoyard*
*Les Haricots verts*
*Les Salsifis à la crème de Ciboulette*

*LA SIXIEME ASSIETTE* — *Le Trianon des Feuilles délicates*
*La Vinaigrette de Framboises*

*LA SEPTIEME ASSIETTE* — *La Tarte de Brie*

*LA HUITIEME ASSIETTE* — *La Corbeille Majestueuse Vigneronne*

*Le Café noir de Colombie*
*La Bonbonnière de Chocolats du Confiseur*

The Petroleum Club of Houston,
under the guidance of General Manager
Erik Worscheh, won "First Place" in
the Special Party Menu Competition
at the Club Managers Association of
America Conference in 1984.

tigious for its tone and refinement. Here was a venue at the top of the city not only for fine dining, but for dancing nightly to a live orchestra. An evening there called for dressing to the hilt because it was a place to see and be seen, and sometimes one even saw royalty the caliber of England's Princess Anne. (Erik was pleased one day to receive a charming letter of appreciation from her Lady in Waiting.)

The view, décor, impeccable service, elegant tableware (gold-plated pace platters, Rosenthal porcelain of cobalt and gold, Baccarat crystal) and entertainment—all contributed to the notion that oil may be a little messy coming out of the ground but it refines into premium grade when raised to the 43rd floor.

Erik made quite an impression at conferences of the Club Managers Association (CMAA). Competing with hundreds of club managers from around the country, he fashioned exhibits depicting special party details, club menus, unique table set-

*Mary and son Mark share Erik's pride at the proclamation he received from the Petroleum Club of Houston.*

tings and his choice of wines to complement each course. It was all second nature to Erik, but fascinating to the judges. He brought back five national trophies honoring his creativity and obvious dedication to the highest standards in his profession.

Back home, he also received satisfaction from his role in gathering research material for a special interest book. It was "The Finest in the Land, the Story of the Petroleum Club of Houston." The author was Jack Donahue, newspaper man and author of 22 books, including seven novels.

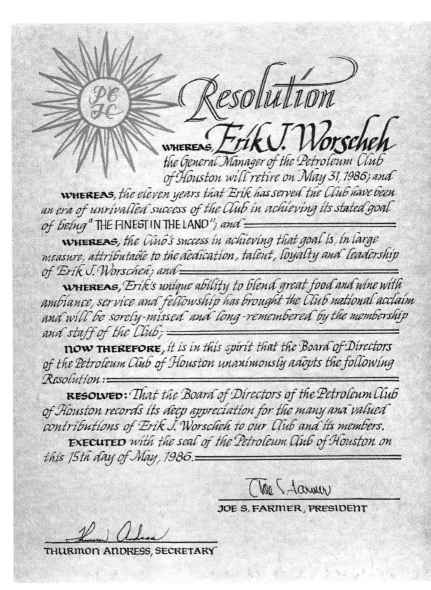

# Resolution

**WHEREAS,** *Erik J. Worscheh* the General Manager of the Petroleum Club of Houston will retire on May 31, 1986; and

**WHEREAS,** the eleven years that Erik has served the Club have been an era of unrivalled success of the Club in achieving its stated goal of being " THE FINEST IN THE LAND"; and

**WHEREAS,** the Club's success in achieving that goal is, in large measure, attributable to the dedication, talent, loyalty and leadership of Erik J. Worscheh; and

**WHEREAS,** Erik's unique ability to blend great food and wine with ambiance, service and fellowship has brought the Club national acclaim and will be sorely-missed and long-remembered by the membership and staff of the Club;

**NOW THEREFORE,** it is in this spirit that the Board of Directors of the Petroleum Club of Houston unanimously adopts the following Resolution:

**RESOLVED:** That the Board of Directors of the Petroleum Club of Houston records its deep appreciation for the many and valued contributions of Erik J. Worscheh to our Club and its members.

**EXECUTED** with the seal of the Petroleum Club of Houston on this 15th day of May, 1986.

**JOE S. FARMER, PRESIDENT**

**THURMON ANDRESS, SECRETARY**

*Upon his retirement as manager of the Petroleum Club, the board and members framed a list of complimentary and appreciative resolutions for Erik and his years of service.*

# Chapter Ten
## The Master's Voice—Escoffier Rules

*I*f Erik Worscheh is unabashedly proud of one of his accomplishments, it would have to be his involvement with *Les Amis d'Escoffier*. Part of that pride comes from replacing unawareness with vast information. He remembers asking a chef why the spectacular dining room atop the Beverly Hilton was called the Escoffier Room. The answer intrigued him to the point of doing in-depth research. Ultimately, that innocent question led to a high point in his career, his being listed as one of the founders of the classic food and wine society in Houston.

Along the way, he not only discovered the "King of the World's Kitchen," but also became a firm disciple of the legendary Frenchman who decreed that cuisine becomes greatest when it honors quality, harmony and simplicity.

Escoffier (1846-1935) had his own hero, French *haute cuisine's* Antoine Careme, but eventually he pared away the fussiness of Careme's elaborate and ornate techniques. Another major influence of Escoffier is extant in today's professional kitchens. He divided the kitchen staff into specialized and disciplined groups, with each complementing the other for fast, efficient production.

Erik calls Escoffier's astonishing book, *"Le Guide Culinaire,"* his bible. Over the years he has used many of its five thousand recipes. He defends his idol against any who would modernize the classic methods. Chinese, Italian, Southwestern cuisines and so forth—all are fine unto themselves, or if one must, can be melded into some kind of fusion invention. But classic is classic, says Erik, and should never fall into the hands of one who likes to tamper.

*Members of the permanent committee of Les Amis d'Escoffier of Houston in 2000*

Typical of Erik's role with the Society was a dinner at the River Oaks Country Club. Joe Mannke, president of the Houston Escoffier Society, brought him to the microphone. It was his pleasure, Mannke said, to introduce the Society's "Godfather," the one who keeps members on a straight and narrow path. He noted that Erik had served as vice president since the Society's founding. Furthermore, he had been involved with every dinner since its founding in 1961.

Then it was Erik's turn. He spoke briefly of the gentleman they all honored. He explained that Escoffier, the original celebrity chef, was an innovator who brought new status to the *chef de cuisine*. Escoffier's principles evolved into certain golden rules which the Society intended to respect. Erik concluded by inviting all the guests to raise their glasses. With his own glass held high, he again offered his celebrated and dramatic toast to Escoffier:

*"The chef of kings and the king of chefs!"*

At the same dinner, Mannke explained what members and guests could expect when one exceptional course followed another, and furthermore, what the exclusive organization expected of them.

There are rules. Even the most sophisticated might not realize that in classic Escoffier ritual, it is useless to say, "Pass the salt and pepper." These condiments, along with butter, are not allowed on the table. Butter is superfluous, having been used generously in preparation, and it is assumed that all seasonings will be no less than perfect as they arrive from the kitchen.

Each course will have its own wine meticulously selected to create a harmonious effect. As the dinner progresses, the array of stems diminishes one by one until the dessert wine signals the winding down of an out-of-the-ordinary evening and a dining experience of the highest rank.

The first gathering of the local *Les Amis d'Escoffier* was early in 1961 while manager Henry O. Barbour was still with the Houston Club. He invited an initial mix of food professionals and other friends and initiated plans for an autumn dinner. Pros included Peter Tomac, Andrew Cipriani, Albert Uster, John Bachmann, Henry Audley, Kurt Ammann, Camille Bermann, Garret Dawson "Sonny" Look, Walter Clist, Frances Wells, Jack Bryant, Charles Finance, Tom Katz and Erik Worscheh.

Today *Les Amis* membership is limited to one hundred persons, fifty percent professionals, twenty-five percent wine and food enthusiasts and twenty-five percent luminaries. The goals are the same as the original society formed by Oscar of the Waldorf in 1936, namely:

*The Les Amis d'Escoffier Society of Houston
Permanent Committee in 2005.*

1. To bring together members of the culinary profession and loyal friends who appreciate good food and wine;
2. To cement the bonds of friendship between members;
3. To acquaint members and the American public with Master Chef and *Cuisenaire* Escoffier and his importance to our culinary institutions and Western culture.

You thought your parents had strict rules at the dinner table? Try these as outlined by Erik Worscheh at *Les Amis d'Escoffier* dinners:

1. An individual may request water, but there is none routinely set at the table.
2. No ash trays, either.
3. There are no bread and butter plates and no salt and pepper shakers (for reasons described above).
4. Silence is required at the serving of each new dish. Thereafter, keep conversation low-key. No politics, please.
5. Men must tuck the napkin into their collars. Women may use the napkin as they see fit.

74

6. The meal will be served at a prescribed time. Begin eating as soon as the food is served.
7. You'll hear a wine commentary, then a food commentary. Because the wine was selected to enhance a particular dish, you'll consume it during the course for which it is intended. Your glass, even if full, will be removed at the end of its course.
8. Only eighty to a hundred reservations will be taken and members must understand that there will be no reserved seats other than for planning committees. Late-comers will begin the meal at whichever course is being served when they arrive.

Note: In Houston, dress tends to be black tie.

Menu planning for each dinner is the responsibility of the host chef. The rule states that he or she must adhere to the standards set by master chef George Auguste Escoffier, with only the slightest deviations to permit use of the best regional seafood available. The selections are subject to full approval of the *Comite de la Bonne Bouche*, the group responsible for planning a particular feast.

Diners may not realize how much advance preparation goes into a dinner of excellence. Months ahead, the planning committee meets with the head chef of the particular hotel, restaurant or club hosting the event. Sometimes the chef is unfamiliar with Escoffier's precise requirements, so Erik—a permanent committee member—has made it a habit to buy the Escoffier "bible" and present it to the host chef. A test dinner is then prepared for committee members, who evaluate all facets of the menu. If, for instance, two dishes are considered too similar in texture, or if the food and wine are judged incompatible, adjustments will be made until the committee is satisfied that the classic principles of Escoffier are satisfied.

* * *

In earlier Houston, steak and barbecue were classy enough to stir the hungry soul. But in January, 1958, Henry O. Barbour, general manager of the private Houston Club, formed "Committee of Four" with three close friends, restaurateurs Camille Bermann, (Maxim's), Andrew Cipriani (Foley's) and Walter Clist (Coronado Club). Later they were joined by Tom Katz and Bob Leroy. Their intention was to promote gracious living, relate wines to fine foods and encourage excellent service. The goals were honorable and nicely publicized, but soon afterwards, Barbour left town and the committee dissolved.

One man did not forget. On June 16, 1976, Erik Worscheh invited a select group of food enthusiasts to a luncheon. Before it was over, a "Committee of Six" formed, complete with guidelines that avoided such formalities as bylaws and dues. Members were Uppy Upshaw, Andrew Cipriani, Ray Watts, Tom Katz, Camille Bermann and Erik. Considering themselves pacesetters, they decreed two luncheons annually in Spring and Fall. Congenial Tom Katz, whose 2K restaurant attracted the after-theater crowd, suggested they also have a festive Yule-Hanukkah Feast of Light dinner to which wives and dates would be invited (as opposed to all other functions for men only). Fine, agreed his friends, and for that excellent idea they appointed him the official Santa Claus.

This group flourished and welcomed new members over the years. These included Fred Parks, Ray Watts, "Red" Steger, Sonny Look, Dick Nelson, Ron Hughes, Pete Sutherland, Gerry Lattin, Horst Manhard, Joe Mannke, Walter Asche, Bob Southwell, Bernard van Mourik, Adriano Farinola, Jack Sorcic and Jim DeGeorge. Still later, Mark Cox, Carmelo Mauro and Alain Le Notre signed up. The numbers kept changing as members moved or passed on—so was it the Committee of Six? Eight? Ten? A solution dawned: the group voted to stop counting and simply call itself "The Committee." In 2006, long-serving Erik passed leadership of the group to Mark Cox, owner of Mark's Restaurant.

Member Fred Parks, a high-profile attorney, owned an impressive private wine cellar. Erik introduced him to the Dean of the University of Houston's Conrad N. Hilton College of Hotel and Restaurant Management. Parks quickly became impressed with the institution's work and potential. Eventually he donated his collection to the college, which then honored him by creating "The Fred Parks Wine Cellar". Today it is an attractive addition to the sophisticated on-campus hotel.

"The Committee" in its various stages was never affiliated with *Les Amis d'Escoffier,* but the two organizations conflated into one mood toward classic cuisine. At last Houston was seeing beyond its limited menu.

And there were other important awakenings. Over time, Erik accepted invitations to join the gourmand societies *Confrerie des Chaine des Rotisseurs,* International Wine & Food Society and the *Confrerie des Chevaliers du Tastevin.* But *Les Amis d'Escoffier* may have topped the others for publicity. Local scribes couldn't resist the glamour, the drama, and the learning experience. Consequently, Erik's scrapbooks bulge with clippings of complimentary stories and cheerful photos.

# Chapter Eleven
## Diplomacy with Celebrities

*L*ong years ago in his halcyon days as a Czechoslovakian schoolboy, Erik Worscheh had dreams of becoming a diplomat. Fate would have it otherwise. But in a sense, the dream was fulfilled if one counts the number of dignitaries and celebrities who have shaken his hand in grateful recognition of his service.

At six-foot-four, Erik stood out in a reception crowd, even when duty required that he step aside and "stand in a corner," as he put it, to evaluate the hotel service operation and spot any need. When called to the fore, he displayed the welcoming smile, the eye contact, the approving words of diplomacy, and photos in his scrapbooks now show that he was a handsome fellow who elicited smiles from the famous.

A few of the renowned guests were marvels of unconventional behavior, but the entire hotel staff was trained to accept eccentricities with calm and exemplary performance.

Erik has met seven presidents of the United States and more celebrities than he can recall in a single conversation. Among the outstanding:

**President Dwight D. Eisenhower:**
As with all presidential visits, security was tight at the Los Angeles Beverly Hilton in advance of Eisenhower's appearance. His saucy First Lady, Mamie, came along for a stay in the Presidential Suite.

Erik had orders straight from the Secret Service to screen all waiters who might work near the dignitaries. Foremost, they needed proof of American citizenship.

Erik finished that task and set about arranging for a memorable dinner. Eisenhower, the former Supreme Commander of the Allied Forces, wasn't interested in a multi-course dinner. He summoned Erik. All he wanted, he said, was a bowl of soup—what could he suggest?

Erik quickly invented an answer. "Mr. President, how about some *Potage Mongol*?

"What is that?"

"It is a cream soup made of green peas and tomatoes with a dash of sherry."

The President agreed. Erik

For Erik Worscheh
with thanks for his courteous service
and best wishes,

Dwight D. Eisenhower

*President Eisenhower*

dashed to the kitchen, only to hear the chef wail, "We don't have any *Potage Mongol*!

"Then make some!" Erik pleaded.

The chef went into double-time.

When the soup was set before the President, he took a couple of analytical sips and shouted to his wife down the table, "Hey, Mamie. This is a hell of a soup. You'd better get some!"

Erik flew back to the kitchen.

For another Eisenhower event, the Hilton's food and beverage director and catering manager, Fred Hayman, asked Erik to dash across the street to L.A.'s posh store, Robinson's. Find an appropriate vessel to hold honey, he was told, because Mamie liked honey in her bourbon. By luck, Erik found the perfect novelty. It was a large and expensive silver bee. By pressing a button, the six-inch insect spread its wings open to reveal a honey pot.

This time it was Mamie who shouted. "Ike, look what I have!" Then to Erik: "May I keep it?" Diplomacy ruled; of course she could keep it.

At a later gathering, Eisenhower motioned to Erik. Apparently remembering the accent, he asked about his home country. Erik told him he was from Bohemia, a historical region of Czechoslovakia. The President then invited him to sit down for a bit of conversation, during which Erik revealed that he looked forward to becoming an American citizen. That information startled the hovering Secret Service. Erik also commented that after World War II his parents and fellow citizens had "waited for General Patton" in hopes their country would not fall into Russian hands. But intricate Yalta and Potsdam plans instead saw Czechoslovakia divided, with Stalin getting a share. A reluctant Patton was forced to turn back only fifty miles from Prague.

Explaining that maneuver to Erik, Eisenhower said, "Son, I had orders from higher ups. It was not my decision."

But under those circumstances, Erik had become a displaced person.

At the end of their friendly chat, Eisenhower asked: "Is there anything I can do for you?"

Erik said he'd be proud to own a photo of the President of the United States.

Back in the hallway, Erik was accosted by the Secret Service. Wasn't he told, they asked sternly, that non-citizens would not be allowed access to the President? After the fact, he was only mildly terrified. "But you said to screen the waiters, and I did," he explained. "You didn't say anything about me!"

A few weeks later, however, he had reason to be alarmed. A telephone call summoned him to the Los Angeles branch of the FBI. *This is it*, thought Erik—*I am being deported.* He quickly made a list of personnel who could replace him and offered it to his puzzled superior. Heavy of heart, he then drove downtown prepared to surrender to the FBI.

Instead, he was asked for his signature by orders of no less than the President of the United States. His jaw dropped when he received a package from the White House. Inside was a photograph with the inscription: "For Erik Worscheh with thanks for his courteous service—best wishes. Dwight D. Eisenhower."

Erik became a naturalized citizen on Oct 4, 1957. He took the occasion to change the spelling of his name. By eliminating the final "c" in Worschech, he decided it would be easier for Americans to pronounce. The simplified version, phonetically, is "Wor-shay."

**Harry S. Truman:**

When former president Truman and his confidante, oil mogul Edwin W. Pauley Sr., announced their plan to have a book debut luncheon for twenty at the Beverly Hilton, Erik set up the menu. As usual, he was on hand to greet the entourage who had come for the introduction of "Year of Decisions— Memoirs of Harry S. Truman."

*Harry S Truman*

"I am pleased to meet you, Mr. Ex President," he said.

Then he wondered why all the guests laughed. One of them kindly explained that, in this country, former presidents are forever-after addressed as "Mr. President." Truman noticed Erik's acute embarrassment.

"That's all right," he said. "You're correct, I am an ex."

At departure, he again addressed Erik, asking him if there was anything he'd like as a memento.

"If you don't mind, Mr. President, I'd love to have one of your books."

There had been nineteen guests and nineteen books. Truman looked around. "Hey, Pauley," he said to his wealthy friend. "You son-of-a-bitch, you don't need a book. Give it to Erik!"

Erik's copy is inscribed "With kind regards to Erik Worscheh from Harry S. Truman, Nov. 28, 1955."

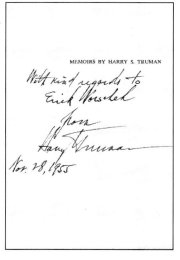

### President Lyndon B. Johnson:

Diplomacy doesn't always work, Erik learned. Prior to a big Shamrock Hilton reception for contributors to the Democratic Party, a smaller group gathered in the International Club Lounge. These were the elite, the individuals who had pledged more than $10,000. President Johnson

*Lyndon Johnson*

walked in with a smile big as Texas and reached out for cordial handshakes. As Johnson approached, Erik welcomed him with appropriate enthusiasm. What was Erik's affiliation, Johnson wanted to know. When Erik said he was with the hotel, the smile vanished quicker than a political contribution. "His face fell flat," remembers Erik, "and he quickly looked away, around the room."

**President Ronald Reagan:**

Manning the banquet office, Erik took a late call at the Beverly Hilton. It was from Nancy Reagan, whose husband was then president of the Screen Actors Guild. She and her Ronny wanted a free private room for a group meeting of the Guild, and they needed it that very evening.

Erik explained that the staff was gone. The Reagans could have the room, but they would have to come over and do the set-up themselves, with his help. That night Reagan, dressed in jeans, Nancy, and Erik worked together to create a long table, then to cover it with cloth, pour ice water, and put chairs in place. In a Houston visit, after Reagan became President, he instantly recognized Erik, saying he remembered him from that hurried occasion and several other functions at the Beverly Hilton.

**President Gerald Ford:**

In Los Angeles, moments before the assembled were to raise their glasses in a toast, Erik murmured into the president's ear that his specially selected wine might suffer a temperature rise if he clutched it in the manner of a gin and tonic. His tactful suggestion: Hold the glass by its stem. Ford seemed appreciative of the lesson, coming as it was from a wine expert.

Erik also served Presidents **Richard Nixon** and **George H. W. Bush** in relatively calm situations. But at the Shamrock Hilton, he encountered election mania when the Kennedy women—**Eunice Shriver** and **Ethel Kennedy (Mrs. Robert)**, with **Lady Bird Johnson**—rolled into town. Their bus displayed a huge banner: "Kennedy Ladies' Reception 1960. Y'all come."

"Y'all" turned out to be nearly four thousand hungry voters-to-be. Charismatic John F. Kennedy was their man and they wanted all to know it. Erik watched his stylish repast of

*George H.W. Bush*

tea and little cakes vanish in minutes. Alarmed, he dispatched his staff to every grocery store near the hotel. Bring back all their cookies and cakes, he ordered. Soon many a shelf was denuded of its sugary delicacies. The Houston press declared the event a huge success, and today Erik's scrapbook contains the business cards of each "Kennedy lady" scribbled with a note of appreciation.

### Howard Hughes:

The enigmatic industrialist, film producer and flyer kept a home in Beverly Hills and also a suite at the Beverly Hilton. During Erik's tenure there, Hughes was already possessed by demon fears of germs. He ordered food at odd hours—dinner in the early morning, breakfast at midnight. He demanded that his waiters be screened for health clearance. They had to wear gloves, and as they entered his quarters, he turned his back on them and faced the window.

### West German Chancellor Ludwig Erhard:

In 1963 Erhard came to the Shamrock Hilton as a guest of Lyndon Johnson, who also invited him to travel on to the Johnson ranch for a weekend Common Market conference and Texas barbecue. Erhard felt somewhat out of place because he did not speak English. Erik to

*Chancellor Ludwig Erhard*

the rescue! He explained in fluent German that Erhard must not refer to Lyndon as "Yonson." He supplied the correct sound.

A grateful Chancellor said, *"Ich bin froh dass Sie mir das gesagt haben."* (I am glad that you told me that.) Then in German he asked Erik, "What is barbecue?"

**Edsel Ford:**

Suites at the Beverly Hilton featured a special bar with a lift-up counter that could be unlatched by pressing a button. Somehow its operation escaped Ford even though he'd listened to an explanation. Erik walked in to find Ford stepping off a chair, then flinging his body over the bar in order to reach bottles from topside. Being the diplomat, Erik offered assistance, but thought privately, *no wonder your Edsel automobile didn't sell!*

**Bob Hope:**

As usual, there was a joke, this one on television. Bob had been to the posh Escoffier Room of the Beverly Hilton. "It was so expensive, they don't even have prices on the menu," he complained. "It was so expensive," he reiterated, "I didn't have enough money to pay the check, and I had to leave my jacket as collateral!"

At one point, Hope took pleasure in walking up and down Hollywood Boulevard while playing with a yo-yo. Said Erik: "He'd drop in at the Beverly Hills Hotel lobby and give the staff yo-yo lessons."

**Fidel Castro:**

When Cuba's Fidel and brother Raul showed up at the Shamrock Hilton, they brought along several companions. Fidel wanted them all accommodated in the same suite where they could continue living within the bonds of communism.

Therefore, he ordered hay brought in so they could sleep on the floor. Fortunately, in those days, hay was easy to find in Houston.

**The heaviest eaters:**

Erik votes for **Henry Kaiser**, the late aluminum king, and **Sid Caesar** of *Your Show of Shows* fame in the '70s. Both big, strong men, they routinely ordered double portions, and in Caesar's case, sometimes more. For breakfast, Erik once suggested to the famous comic that he might enjoy a Beverly Hilton specialty, petite loin lamb chops. Caesar asked how many chops in a serving. "Two," replied Erik. The little chops were quite expensive.

"Bring me fourteen of them," ordered Caesar.

His breakfast would cost him about $200.

**Del Webb**, renowned real estate developer:

When a breakfast order arrived from his seventh floor suite, the chef knew it meant two poached eggs. They had to be cooked exactly right, or they'd be sent back. After many tries, the morning chef finally worked out a routine. He'd poach two eggs in boiling water, then at the precise time, he lifted them out and plopped them down on a stainless steel side table. If the eggs popped up like a ping pong ball and the yolks did not break, they were just right. Next he placed them on toast, nestled the order under a glass dome and rushed it up to the Del Webb suite for calm, matter-of-fact presentation by the captain.

**Frank Sinatra:**

Erik met the Rat Pack (Sinatra, Sammy Davis Jr., Dean Martin, Peter Lawford and Joey Bishop) at a club in Las Vegas and later at the Beverly Hilton. As the recipient of Erik's usual gracious attentions, Sinatra asked that question: "What would you like to have?" Erik hesitated. Sinatra saved him the trouble. "Here, take this," he said, and pulled an expensive watch off his wrist. It's still among Erik's mementos.

**Conrad Hilton:**

Guests invited to special luncheons and dinners at the Hilton mansion in Bel Air might have wondered how the events proceeded so smoothly through various courses without a word from the host to his staff. Erik, often summoned to the events along with members of the highly-trained Beverly Hilton staff, tells the secret. It was a traffic light system discreetly controlled by buttons under the table where the host sat. When Hilton pressed the yellow button, it flashed in the service entrance and meant "Get Ready." Green signaled "Serve." Red called for "Pick up," meaning plates and silverware were to be removed from the table after each course.

**Col. Henry Crown:**

The Crowns, noted for their immense wealth and philanthropy in Chicago, not to mention ownership of the Empire State Building until 1961, maintained a top floor suite at the Beverly Hilton, next to Howard Hughes. The Hiltons and Crowns were close friends; it was the Colonel who influenced Conrad's maneuvers when he bought the Palmer House in Chicago and the Waldorf-Astoria in New York City.

Erik's experience with the Chicago couple mainly involved Mrs. Crown, who insisted that meals be served with extreme care. She had her floors covered with pristine white carpets and she insisted they be kept exactly that way. Erik therefore answered her summons in the company of a strong-armed waiter who could hoist and balance the entire rolling cart and its contents over his head. He walked ever so carefully over the carpets and deposited the load on the Crown's uncarpeted balcony.

And so many others...

Because hotels featured famous musicians as their entertainment, Erik met such as **Judy Garland** and **Lisa Minnelli.** He served royalty, namely **Princess Anne of England,** and also England's **Prime Minister Margaret Thatcher and Prime Minister Clement Atlee;** also, **Field Marshal B. L. Montgomery,** who attended a function at March Air Force Base and stopped at the Mission Inn.

A bona fide diplomat couldn't boast of a more copious list of extraordinary encounters. Or put another way, Erik was just doing his job.

# Chapter Twelve
## An Interlude for Health

O ne of Erik's and Mary's greatest challenges was beginning to unfold. The story of their triumph and recovery deserves to be told.

In 1986, the Petroleum Club of Houston's board of directors asked Erik to retire because, for the second time, he was exhibiting symptoms of alcohol abuse. First, though, respecting his years of service, they would finance his rehabilitation at a Florida institution. Upon his return, he would sign off with a pension. It was the board's feeling that this treatment would be more effective if Erik wasn't constantly surrounded by the club's huge assortment of temptations.

Mary went along to Florida. "I may be drinking a little too much, too," she told the director of the clinic. Test results showed that her problem wasn't as severe as her husband's, but bad enough to enroll in the treatment program.

Their first attempt at recovery in 1981 had failed because Erik and Mary became complacent about the program and carelessly resumed drinking. Erik remembers ruefully: "I only had that one glass of wine at dinner, but soon I had fifteen hidden around the house." He describes alcoholism as a terrible craving that would waken him in the middle of the night with the overwhelming need for a drink.

How did it start? Now recognized as a disease, alcoholism has another facet. A recent study supports the idea of genetic vulnerability. Looking back, Erik remembered that Papa had the same problem back in those days when he so often "checked the temperature" in the wine cellar and stayed too long. Erik believes he inherited the tendency. His brother Walter did not and Mutti could take a sip of wine without craving another.

Perhaps if the Worschehs, like many others in the profession, hadn't been exposed to so much alcohol, they would not have fallen prey. Erik had traveled a long road to acquire the vast knowledge of a much-admired wine connoisseur. In a blind tasting, he could recognize the country, region and year of a wine—an astonishing accomplishment. In addition to formal tastings, there were years of cocktail parties, home entertaining and fancy dinners where each course paired with a special wine. Informally, there also were the wine salesmen who showed up in his office with a new bottle and an eager invitation. "Erik! Come, you have to try this one!" And in Mary's case, on those long evenings while she waited for her husband to finish work, it seemed appropriate to relax with a glass of wine, or more. When she accompanied him for special events, her drinking did not stand out—drinking was fashionable; everyone had a favorite cocktail in those days, or so it seemed. In fact, some individuals who abstained were known to hide the fact, perhaps by sipping water and calling it vodka.

"I never got a DWI," said Erik, but recalled that he fell asleep in his car one night on his way home. A policeman awakened him. The officer believed Erik's story that he was suffering from extreme fatigue and waved him on.

The reason the Worschehs want their story known is, first, they each have attained 21 years of sobriety. They are staunch believers in the power of intervention by caring family or friends. In Erik's case, he had been approached by an individual who himself was a recovering alcoholic. Ever since the Worschehs accepted the Alcoholics Anonymous 12-step program for recovery, they've been preaching AA's gospel of sobriety, how to get there, how to stay there and how to help others recognize their own needs.

The program gave them the tools and knowledge they needed to stay in healthy recovery. They learned that such a state of health depends on personal honesty—letting go of self-deception and facing up to character flaws and then making amends. Of utmost importance was learning to "live in the moment," letting go of yesterday and not dwelling on tomorrow.

Erik and Mary are grateful for the support they received during the 1980s from two dear friends who are now deceased, Pat Flynn and Father John DeForest.

Another source of inspiration, then and now, is the Council on Alcohol and Drugs Houston. Among other leading citizens to form this group in 1946 were R.E. Bob Smith, Oveta Culp Hobby and Bishop Clinton Quinn, with immediate success. That year the Council assisted 56 people, but probably couldn't imagine the number in the year 2003 when it served 263,000 men, women and children.

Erik's dedicated service on the board of the Council and his voluntary work have earned him the title of honorary lifetime member. Inspired by his dedication, Mary volunteered with the organization and later became a member of its advisory board. She has worked with the Council's on-site medical clinic, K.I.N.D.E.Rx Clinic Houston. It provides health care for substance-exposed children from birth (with fetal alcohol syndrome or drug exposure symptoms) to age 20. Currently over a thousand individuals are under Clinic care. Mary has actively sought grants from local organizations for this important community endeavor.

Was it a predetermined course that the Worschehs would turn from a personal disaster toward good works for others? They don't believe in such a lofty purpose. They know that "recovered" alcoholics aren't actually recovered, that the weakness is a fact and temptation lurks in unexpected places. The struggle gets easier over the years, but the disease of alcoholism is forever and those afflicted must never let their guard down. Erik and Mary learned that reaching out and helping others is insurance for "staying the course" one day at a time.

# Chapter Thirteen
## This is Retirement?

*R*etirement—a magic word or a long sentence? For Erik, a stranger to boredom, retirement meant freedom to explore, to meet a host of new people and turn them into instant friends.

Once he and Mary set a determined course on a healthy non-alcoholic lifestyle, their world unfolded like the blossoms of spring. In 1986, soon after leaving the Petroleum Club, Erik joined the Worrell Design Group as a consultant and associate. The firm concentrates on kitchens and dining rooms of hotels, restaurants, clubs, hospitals, universities and corporations. A natural!

Rodney Worrell, president, appreciated that Erik anchored his creative ideas to solid practicality. The commercial kitchen had been Erik's home-away-from-home. He knew well that, unlike the cozy and decorative residential sort, it must function for long hours each day. It must accommodate staffs of fast, foot-weary, demanding, sometimes emotional food experts. In other words, things had better be handy and workable.

*Rodney Worrell, May C. Boitel, director of public relations for Worrell Design Group, with Mary and Erik at a dinner held at the Conrad Hilton College.*

All through his service career, from hotels in Bohemia, California, Nevada and Texas, Erik had accumulated operative knowledge the way a bee gathers pollen. During one period, he had worked as consultant with another design group, Mulhauser-McCleary. One of that firm's projects involved helping the University of Houston's College of Hotel and

Restaurant Management with its banquet kitchen setup and the student lab kitchen. A key man in the organization at that time was Rodney Worrell, who later bought the company, gave it his name, and figured prominently in Erik's life.

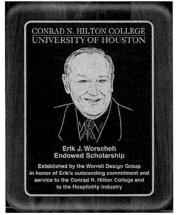

On another occasion, when Juan Cortina of a prominent Mexico City banking family and his numerous business associates chose Houston for a grandiose restaurant, Erik made practical suggestions. They were put into practice when the businessman's son, architect Juan Cortina, reproduced Mexico City's colonial La Hacienda de los Morales

*A plaque displayed at the University of Houston's Conrad Hilton College recognizes the Erik J. Worscheh endowed scholarship established by the Worrell Design Group.*

on twenty acres of then-remote west Houston. Unfortunately, the exquisite restaurant did not flourish. It has been replaced by upscale apartments adjacent to the Sam Houston Tollway near Buffalo Bayou.

But the Juan Cortina-Worscheh friendship lingered on. A high point was Cortina's invitation to Erik, Mary and Mark, and their friends, Edith and Harry Patterson and son Bruce, to vacation at his idyllic home in Cuernavaca. They were picked up by a limo, driven to a hacienda complete with pool, a housekeeper and meals served on a picture-pretty veranda. At one of the luncheons, they were joined by well-known Houstonians Appellate Court Judge J. Curtiss Brown and Mrs. (Lovice) Brown.

As a consultant, Erik was not concerned with purchase of kitchen appliances; rather, he had a keen eye for function and

*Eric Hilton, Erik Worscheh, Barron Hilton and Mary Worscheh at the University of Houston's Conrad N. Hilton College of Hotel and Restaurant Management. The party was for Barron's induction into the school's Hall of Honor.*

arrangement. He frowned at any awkward juxtaposition of kitchen and service area, or a large dining room that could not be reorganized into smaller (lucrative) sections by movable walls. The latter had been a difficulty at La Hacienda—Cortina had imported spectacular antique chandeliers. They were gorgeous but so large that they made reconfiguration of dining room walls impossible.

Also during this period, the boards of The Briar Club of Houston and the Houston Yacht Club took note of Erik's retirement. They sent out a call for his temporary assistance while they searched for permanent managers. In each case, he accepted the position and also shared his knowledge of possible candidates.

\* \* \*

But consulting was not always a full-time job. There were other things to do, places to go. Frequently Erik and Mary packed their bags to visit friends in Germany. In Munich, a special friend and classmate, Renate von Pauer, and her husband, Claus, offered the use of their historic lakeside home on Ammersee. A lasting memory: each morning the housekeeper took an early bicycle trip to the village baker and brought back fragrant rolls and bread for breakfast. The home became a hub for excursions during the Worschehs' stay. Back in Houston, they were able to reciprocate twice on separate occasions. Both Claus and daughter Nikki became patients at the

Texas Medical Center for successful heart surgery and spent time with the Worschehs.

Side trips to Munich and Nuremberg also gave Erik, the man with an ever-ready handshake and broad smile, opportunities for merry reunions over the years with other old college friends from the University of Nuremberg. A get-together even occurred in the United States.

One former classmate was Willy Frank who had moved to Hammondsport, N.Y., following his father, Dr. Konstantin Frank, of the Ukraine. The elder Frank had already made history here by

*Mary and Erik visiting a University of Houston function. A scholarship to the hotel and restaurant management school has been named in his honor.*

*A gathering of old friends, Erik, Willy Frank and Dr. Hansl Popp in the tasting room of the renowned Dr. Konstantin Frank winery in New York's Finger Lakes region.*

successfully grafting French and German vines to New York and Canadian specimens. His accomplishment amazed wine lovers who were convinced that the region's harsh winters froze out any useful possibilities other than Mogen David and Taylor brands. Willy and his wife Margrit took on duties at his father's famous Vinifera Wine Cellars and vineyards in the Finger Lakes Region.

In 2004, Willy and Margrit invited the Worschehs and their

*Willy and Margrit Frank, Ruth and, Hansl Popp at Dr. Popp's 80th birthday party, a lavish event on Mallorca.*

mutual friends, Dr. Hansl Popp and his wife Ruth, for a reunion in Hammondsport. Being the first time they had been together since college days, it was an exceptional week for the gentlemen.

But the very next year, there they were, together again! This time the instigation came from Hansl Popp, who decided that his 80th birthday would not go unnoticed—to put it mildly. When the invitation came, Erik and Mary marked off two weeks on their calendar for a rush of European activities, crowned by the lavish Popp celebration on beautiful Mallorca, a Mediterranean island off the coast of Spain.

Popp and family made their fortune in natural healing products which are widely appreciated in Europe. Their company, Bionorica, is headquartered in Germany with a division on Mallorca, along with their vineyards, medicinal plants and laboratories. These days the complex is managed by the Popps' son, Michael, who opened the doors for a look-see by the birthday entourage.

While it was hard to leave the comforts and view of their small hacienda, S'Olivaret, near the Sierra de Tramuntana, Erik

*Standing in front of history: Erik and Mary with Mallorca's ancient gothic Catedral de Palma in the background.*

and Mary happily joined the other guests (40 in all from Germany, Switzerland and Italy) for tours, dining and celebrations. Easily the most memorable was a visit to a castle built by Archduke Ludwig Salvator. He was an Austrian aristocrat who championed Mallorca's wildlife before conservation was a popular consideration. (Actor Michael Douglas bought some of his scenic property.) The castle overlooks the jagged coastline and is said to capture Mallorca's most beautiful sunsets. Guests were seated in its massive music room for a concert of classical pieces played on two grand pianos.

On the final evening, everyone piled into a bus for a winding trip to the top of a mountain, site of the winery and adjacent Castell Miquel, Michael's addition to the family holdings. Coats and wraps felt good during the champagne reception on a veranda that overlooks breathtaking scenery. At a signal, the marveling guests moved into the aromatic winery. Enough space had been cleared among huge silver vats for a massive U-shaped table. Besides a catered dinner, the party-goers were treated to a video of Hansl's life. He accepted congratulatory remarks with a speech of his own in which he expressed gratitude for his "two dear friends and their wives" who came all way from the U.S.A. to honor his birthday. By this time, having experienced days of royal treatment, Erik and Mary felt certain the honor was all theirs.

In March of 2007, they had an opportunity to do a little reciprocal hosting. Another Popp family business is the manufacture of specialty gift-wrapping paper at Neustadt/Coburg, north of Nuremberg. It was founded by Ruth's father. An accomplished artist, Ruth designed patterns which have appealed to customers throughout Europe and soon may be marketed in the United States. With that mission in mind, the Popps' son Juergen, president of the company, and his wife, Ute, vice president of marketing, visited potential clients in Dallas and Oklahoma. They flew into

Houston especially for a whirlwind sight-seeing tour, with Mary and Erik as their eager guides.

* * *

Back home, Erik's retirement took on many dimensions. Several times a year, he drove across town to answer a call from the University of Houston's hotel school. His mission was to lecture budding hoteliers and restaurateurs on his favorite subject, the essentials of good service in the hospitality field. Quite often professionals still greet him with an enthusiastic handshake and a typical introduction, "I was in your class, Mr. Worscheh!" He loves the feedback. And he is proud to have worked with a succession of deans at the school, namely James Taylor, interim dean Douglas Keister, Gerald Lattin, interim dean Clinton L. Rappole, Joseph Cioch, Hugh Walker, Alan Stutts, interim Dean Agnes DeFranco and John Bowen.

Mary's energy, meanwhile, spilled out of the house. While Erik was still at the Petroleum Club, she had challenged herself to learn the ins and outs of the real estate residential field. That meant she was working while Erik engaged in some serendipitous adventures. They went in two directions, one a dignified group association, and the other a bit of madness that had Mary shaking her head in wonder.

Already active in many food and wine groups, he joined a completely different kind of organization. This was the Silver Fox Advisors, retired and semi-retired executives. Their aim was to share their accumulated business wisdom with the less experienced. They offered advice and encouragement, or if the prospects for success looked dim, they saved the would-be entrepreneur thousands of dollars by revealing inevitable risks. Erik credits Gerald de Shrenck Sill, an international hotelman, and William J. (Bill) Spitz, a management expert, for his involvement.

Back in the seventies, Madeline O'Brien encouraged Mary to join a new chapter of the Theresians of the United States (now international). Declaring that sometimes spirituality and theology can be stifling to ordinary souls, this organization encourages "communities" of about thirty women to cut through complexities and define their faith in simple, straight-forward terms. Father Michael Alchediak of Strake Jesuit School became the first sponsor and guided that process at monthly meetings in various members' homes. The result for Mary was a number of priceless and enduring friendships. Another influence has been the Charity Guild of Catholic Women. Mary's membership was sponsored by Marjorie Spring and Rosalind Robertson in 1996. Since then, she has been active in the Guild's resale shop at 1203 Lovett Blvd, and recently because of health responsibilities, has become an associate member. The Guild supports health-related organizations for children in need anywhere in the Greater Houston area. Through the work and support of volunteer members, it has achieved in excess of $1 million in gross sales.

After Mark left to make a life of his own, Mary and Erik moved to a two-story town home in Hammersmith, west of the Galleria. For the next fifteen years, Erik served as vice president of the homeowners association. He headed the swimming pool committee and championed the purchase of safety steps for handicapped residents. They should be able to enjoy the pool, too, he argued, knowing how much he liked relaxing poolside. Before long he met almost everyone in the tree-lined community.

To Mary's amazement, it is rare that they exit their home without someone (usually female) calling, "Hello, Erik!" He explains this by noting that Mary is rather reserved about meeting strangers, while he is the opposite and can always find something to say.

Good enough, but Erik still had time on his hands. "Ah ha," he said to himself one day. "I will reorganize the refrigerator. I'll show Mary how it should be done. She'll save time and steps, and won't always be standing there looking for things."

He removed everything from the appliance. He then replaced items in logical order by category (condiments as a group, etc.). Those seldom used were assigned to the back of shelves.

"She had everything upside down," he complained. Next, affixing tape to the inside wall of the fridge, he labeled each shelf's assignment. The process took analytical thought based on long professional experience and effective procedure in commercial settings.

Then Mary came home from work with her arms full. She had stopped at a supermarket on the way. Erik watched expectantly as his beloved opened the refrigerator. He awaited her surprise, then her delight with his thoughtful workmanship. Not so. By habit, she quickly shoved her purchases in wherever they fit. He had to ask: Hadn't she noticed the logic of her devoted husband's handiwork? His gift of spare time through method and order?

"Nonsense," she said.

Erik summed up his lasting defeat with a lament. "She just didn't understand."

That's not to say Erik's keen sense of order isn't prevalent elsewhere in the house. The kitchen may belong to Mary, but upstairs on specially constructed shelves are books, many thick scrapbooks and records and copies of records. Mary figures the shelves hold up to forty briefcases. Their contents represent all the components of Erik's many-faceted life. And they are organized—his way.

# Chapter Fourteen
## Opposing Memories

*I*t's one thing to accumulate fond memories on a trip and quite another to collect disturbing sights that haunt a traveler for the rest of his life.

Erik had both enthusiasm and misgivings about seeing Jechnitz again. He knew his childhood home had changed. He couldn't imagine how much.

In 1990, Bohemia was opened to outsiders for the first time since the Communists claimed it as a World War II prize. Anxious to see his old home again and to at last show Mary where he grew up, Erik made elaborate plans. First they would visit Walter in Germany, then cross the border for a look. Mark, already visiting Europe, joined his parents—he, too, was curious about the idyllic land he had so often heard his father describe.

They rented a car and headed for Prague. That night their hotel room, hardly a luxury, cost $300. They also paid for their ration of gasoline coupons at the hotel, which gave them access to one of only two operating stations with unleaded gasoline —if access is the correct word for a two-mile line of customers. There were other stations available, but none carried the preferred fuel.

Then on to Jechnitz for a view of the lake where Erik and Walter had ice skated freely as youngsters. To his astonishment, Erik saw a fence at water's edge. Clearly, people were no longer welcome at any season.

So many houses on the way appeared long ago abandoned. Roofs caved in. Yards, once palettes of bold flowers, had turned dull and bare after years of neglect.

As the visitors drove down the main street toward the hotel, Erik eagerly described what Mark and Mary would see.

The elegant boulevard, he said, was a presentation of stones which had been laid by hand in impressive patterns—a sight to remember. But when they made the turn, Eric was stunned. The elegance had been converted to a plain dirt road. Later he questioned a resident, a school teacher, who explained that a sewer line had been installed ten years earlier and all the excavated dirt was simply piled over the artful avenue. There it stayed, in all its communist austerity.

The worst shock was the hotel. It still stood there, but all its doors and windows recoiled behind old boards as if it were blindfolded against any vestige of human activity. In back, where Papa had his butcher shop, Erik saw several unsmiling Ukrainians who had made living quarters of the ground floor space. They appeared frightened at the sight of well-dressed strangers, perhaps fearing they would be evicted.

Even the graveyard behind the hotel was gone. It had been paved over and turned into a parking lot for a drive-in movie. And the Catholic church where the Worschehs once worshipped—Erik remembered hearing that the priest had simply disappeared when Communists took over. The invaders boarded up its stained-glass windows, expressing their own dark view of religion by shutting out the sun.

Everywhere it was the same. The railroad station where Erik had said his good-bye to Papa was now dirty and ugly. Once-immaculate farm homes appeared to be sinking, their shutters hanging askew. The bakery, the butcher shop—in Erik's words, all junk.

Mary and Mark were fascinated by a country that had been hidden so long from Western view and were curious and willing to see more, but it was too much for Erik. In the space of a few hours, depressing reality tarnished any thoughts of his happy childhood. Now there would always be two hotels, one a pleasant dream, the other a nightmare. In front of his family, Erik lowered his head into his hands and cried.

# Chapter *Fifteen*
## Roses in December

*"God gave us memory so that we might have
roses in December."*—James M. Barrie

*A*t this writing in early 2007, Erik Worscheh is 84 years
old and meeting life head-on despite some physical
challenges. Mary hovers nearby, so ready to assist that
she seems to have a dozen hands. They reach decisions by spir-
ited debate, but in the most loving way. It's been a long and
rewarding marriage.

They collect friends. Cards come in the mail expressing
appreciation for some deed or other performed by the
Worschehs. Open the front door of their fashionable condominium and one may well find a package of cookies left by a
neighbor. The telephone jangles and someone wants to share
news or remind them of a meeting or a special dinner. The
instrument invariably holds a new spate of messages recorded
in the hours they were away from home.

But while they look ahead to activities, memories sweeten
their days. As proof, walls and tabletops bear up under dozens
of photographs—young smiles and old ones, famous faces and
the dear ones of family.

*Time flies over us, but leaves its shadow behind.*
—Nathaniel Hawthorne

In 1958, military orders sent Erik's sister Margit and her
Air Force husband Jimmy to live in Orly, France. They invited Mutti and Papa to share their quarters because, by this
time, the elders had retired from the restaurant business.

On March 9, 1959, Margit called Erik with the sorrowful news that Papa, at age 73, had died at home. Grief-stricken, Erik had to tell her he couldn't attend his father's funeral on such short notice because of an especially demanding schedule at the Shamrock Hilton Hotel.

He learned that Mutti wanted the burial to be in a cemetery at Ansbach, Germany, where they had a family plot, but crossing the border without many required legal documents related to the death would be time-consuming and extremely difficult. Margit and Jimmy promised they would handle arrangements as best they could.

Later Erik heard the details. Jimmy drove the car and Margit sat beside him. In back sat Mutti and Papa—they had propped his body up as if he were a living passenger. The drive from Paris to Ansbach was long, arduous and harrowing. When they finally reached the border check point, a guard peered into their windows and assumed he was looking at an old man dozing off. He waved the car through.

Alfred Worschech was born in 1887 in Tepel-Egerland, Bohemia, Austrian-Hungarian Monarchy. Erik remembers him as a flamboyant greeter at the "front of the house" in the hotel and restaurant business—a trait he was most fortunate to inherit.

\* \* \*

Erik's Mutti, Franziska Worschech nee Buresch, was born on Jan, 10, 1894 in Kaschitz, Bohemia, Austrian-Hungarian Monarchy. Her siblings were Rosa, Mary and Josef Pepp. Mutti became a citizen of Czechoslovakia after World War I when the country was created by the Versailles Agreement. She worked for families of nobility as a governess and in various jobs for the Royal Family of the Austrian Empire. She enjoyed poetry and music as well as creating fine dinners at the Worschech Hotel in Jechnitz, Bohemia. Because they were German speaking, Mutti and Papa were expelled from CSR (Czechoslovak Socialist Republic) by the communists after World War II. They became refugees in Germany, living in Ansbach. As a widow, Mutti lived with daughter Margit, son-in-law Jimmy Fox and their four children at various times and in several countries, depending on where the U.S.A.F. assigned Jimmy. Her final mailing address was Virginia Beach, VA. She died at age 92 on Feb. 3, 1987, in the Naval Hospital of Portsmouth, VA.

\* \* \*

Margit Worschech Fox, born Feb. 20, 1926, in Jechnitz, Bohemia, CSR, escaped from behind the Iron Curtain after World War II. Margit was gifted in languages, speaking four fluently and understanding seven. Her talent led to a job as a translator in Ansbach at the Allied Military Headquarters and eventually to the love of her life. She met and dated Capt. James Fox, U.S.A.F., in 1947. He sponsored her emigration to America and they were married in his hometown, New Rochelle, NY, in 1948. Their first move, to Riverside, CA, was the beginning of a series of transfers by the U.S.A.F.—to Nova Scotia, Spain, France, Turkey and back to the U.S. They retired in Virginia. Margit and Jim had four children, Jennifer, Jonathan, Jessica and Jeff. Jimmy died on Feb.14, 1995. Margit died on Nov. 28, 1997, of cancer.

\* \* \*

Most of the American establishments where Erik worked are still standing, but one notable place is long gone in the tradition of an ever-changing, always-bulldozing city. Even though Glenn McCarthy's fabulous Shamrock Hotel added the glitzy name "Hilton" to its identity, it was not immune to Houston's lack of sentiment. During Erik's stay, glamour and fun reigned with a new sophistication and dignity. Then suddenly in 1986 it was over. The hotel was sold and razed, leaving only the convention hall and the garage. The property now belongs to the burgeoning Texas Medical Center.

\* \* \*

Immediately after World War II, German-speaking Bohemians were targets and communist bullets were all too ready. Erik's brother, Walter, finished with service in the German Air Force (as a draftee), gave a false address, saying he lived in Selb, Germany. That would put him near the border, as close as he dared be to his former home. He wore a white band, which indicated "neutral." But temptation was too great—he crossed the border for a long denied reunion with his parents and sister in Jechnitz. He found them in a little house where they had taken tenuous refuge after being ousted from the family hotel. Had he been discovered there, he would have been shot. When Communist inspectors knocked on the door, Mutti hid him under the bed.

Two days later, Margit and a friend managed to get Walter back on a train to Selb. He found a job but income could not erase his profound and debilitating loneliness at Christmas time. Neighbors took pity and brought him food. Not until the next year, when Margit escaped to Selb and found him, did his spirits revive. And the sun shone even brighter when Mutti and Papa came by train. They told of having slept on straw as they traveled in the tightly packed cattle car. Mutti also revealed that diamonds she had bought over the years, planning to pass them on to her children, were lost forever. She had kept them hidden until expulsion was inevitable; then she spoke to a Czech policeman whom she had known and trusted for many years. He graciously offered to protect her treasures and return them when she got settled. Later she attempted to contact him, but she never saw or heard from him again.

Margit got her parents settled as refugees in Leutershausen nearby. The turn-around had begun. Walter, feeling secure at last, entered a field that was in its early stage of development. Computers would be his career, which eventually lifted him to a

*In 1992, Walter came from his home in Germany to tour the U.S. Here he reunites with brother Erik, left, and sister Margit.*

top position with the Bavarian Light Company. By his retirement in 1983, as special assistant to the CEO, he was overseer to 34 specialists.

In his early eighties now and a resident at a senior citizens establishment, Walter finds great enjoyment looking at the scenery, and what a view! Another pleasure is the afternoon *Kuchen* and *Kaffee* in the adjoining hotel garden restaurant. The home is on the outskirts of Munich at Herrsching on the Ammersee. Walter's third-floor quarters include a large balcony which in one direction overlooks a peaceful lake and in another, the magnificent Alps.

Peaceful—but in the spring of 2007 came a flurry of activity. Telephones rang all around with an urgent message from Walter to friends in Germany and relatives from Bohemia now living in Germany. The Worschehs were coming for a visit!

Erik and Mary made the decision to travel after considerable concern about his health. Walking was difficult to be sure, but Erik's determination made up in strength for what

*Erik's 2007 trip to Germany not only gave him a much anticipated reunion with brother Walter, at left, but also a meeting with Cristl Piller, a childhood friend of theirs in Czechoslovakia.*

his legs lacked. The two of them consulted doctors and family. All agreed that a reunion of the two elderly brothers, possibly their last one, would be exhilarating, even restorative.

Excited by the news, Walter and his friend Anne made reservations for a two-week period at Andechser Hof Hotel, a small establishment adjoining his retirement home, but it was his plan that the hotel would only serve as headquarters. There were places to go, people to meet.

The Worschehs left Houston on May 27 and upon arrival in Germany were thrust headlong into an incredible schedule of luncheons and trips to various lakeside restaurants in the picturesque countryside between Munich and the Alps.

The first Saturday, twenty-six old school friends and some relatives showed up in the hotel's private dining room. They included Dr. Hansl and Ruth Popp from Nurnberg, and Renate von Pauer of Munich. Erik had kept in touch with them over the years, but Hansl and Renate, living in the same country, hadn't seen each other for 55 years. In no time their college experiences at the University of Nurnberg came alive again in stories that had everyone laughing. The luncheon brought relatives from points in Germany, among them cousins Renate Rack and husband Gerhard, and daughter, Melina of Wurzburg, and Ursula Schwag of Munich; and Hannelore Francke and husband Hans, from Burgkirchen.

*In 2007, Erik and Mary traveled to Germany for a reunion with Walter and many friends. Seated here, they are shown with members of the Von Pauer family, left to right, Nicoletta, Renate and Nikki.*

Walter's surprises the second Saturday were more relatives for another luncheon at the hotel. Included were Dr. Klaus and Eva Weber, Bernhard and Anna Mueller and their daughter Karin and her husband, Stephan Reichenwallner, and friends Dr. Liska and Professor Juergen Kroner. Then on they went to the Weber home in Feldafing on StarnbergerSee for dessert and a concert by talented cousin Karin, who sang several classical songs. She was accompanied by Dr. Weber on the piano.

Not a day went by that there wasn't a special occasion with a special view and a torrent of memories about Jechnitz, the family hotel and long-gone days as children in Bohemia. Especially poignant was a reunion with a childhood friend, Christl Piller, whom Erik had not seen in nearly 65 years. For Erik and Mary, the trip was a treasure, thanks to Walter and enduring brotherly love.

The Worschehs returned to Houston exhausted but also invigorated. For Erik, it was the satisfaction of having made the right decision, in this case despite doubts about his physical well-being. As it turned out, matters dearest to his heart triumphed over disabilities caused by diabetes.

During the previous years, there had been numerous problems associated with aging—knee and hip replacements, implantation of a pacemaker, development of macular degeneration—but Erik's diabetes took a serious turn in 2000. Poor circulation in the extremities (peripheral vascular disease) and nerve damage (neuropathy) made wound healing in the feet and legs a real challenge. Quite often such conditions lead to amputation.

Luckily, Erik discovered the Center for Wound Healing at Memorial Hermann Hospital in the Texas Medical Center. Its director, Dr. Caroline Fife, and her staff, including Dr. Erik Maus, put up a mighty defense against amputation. With their continuing expertise and Mary's home nursing, Erik so far has escaped the feared extreme results. Significantly, in 2001, Dr. R.W. Smalling, Cardiovascular Surgeon at Memorial Hermann Hospital, performed angioplasty below the left knee, a procedure many surgeons shunned at that time. Its success enabled immediate and on-going treatment.

In his lifetime, Erik Worscheh has traveled a long road from once-idyllic Bohemia to horrors of war, to a new land and a shaping of purpose. By the time he reached Texas, he had experienced emotions ranging from acute despair and sorrow to warm pleasure, excitement and contentment. His successes over the years seem to represent a practical philosophy described by William Barclay:

"We will often find compensation if we think more of what life has given us and less about what life has taken away."

# About the Author

Beverly Harris interviewed Erik Worscheh countless times in order to augment his crisp outline intended as a memoir for his wife Mary and family. The interviews revealed a gamut of experiences in war and peace, sorrow, love, career challenges, and, not the least, humor.

Harris began her career in journalism at Houston's neighborhood Citizen newspapers, then moved on to the *Houston Post*, *Riverside Press Enterprise* (Calif.) and *Houston Chronicle*. After her retirement, she and Emma Lee Turney co-authored *Denim and Diamonds*, which tells how Turney transformed tiny Round Top, Texas, into a mecca for hunters of antiques. Harris was born in that German-speaking town with its population of fewer than 100 quiet citizens and was thrilled at age nine to move to bustling Houston, which boasted two magnificent skyscrapers and three daily newspapers. Still in Houston, she long ago lost count of its myriad skyscrapers, and in writing this book, she and the Worschehs have enjoyed reminiscing about the city's defining events and personalities.